ENVIRONMENT
LAW AND JUSTICE

M.A.A. BAIG

Regency Publications
New Delhi 110 008

ISBN 81-86030-27-1

Published by Regency Publications, 20/36-G, Old Market, West Patel Nagar, New Delhi 110 008 and printed at Radiant Printers, New Delhi, Phones: 571 3968, 578 3571.

6

ENVIRONMENT LAW AND JUSTICE

PREFACE

I had been thinking to write a book since the Supreme Court's judgement, to keep environmental education as a compulsory subject, at all levels in the educational institutions, has becn pronounced. This book is based entirely on the idea of making environmental education compulsory.

Nevertheless, it will be of immense benefit to lawyers, jurists, judges, legislators, executives, environmentalists and infact everyone. Chapter VI of the book specifically and elaborately deals with environmental education. The book can be prescribed both at the LL.B. and LL.M. levels. Besides, this can also be prescribed for courses in Science and Social Science subjects.

All legislations and judicial decisions relating to environmental protection can be referred to in this book. Uptodate legislation and judicial decisions have been discussed in this book.

I am thankful to my publisher for having accepted my manuscript for publication.

Berhampur, Orissa
December 1, 1995

Dr. M.A.A. Baig

Contents

INTRODUCTION

Local habitat issues related to the cleanliness and wholesomeness of the surroundings, the denudation of hills and mountains of their tree cover and subsequent loss of soil mantle etc. have been noted and lamented by writers since time immemorial. But the perception of global environmental issues seems to be of recent origin. As Caldwell (1984) puts it:

> "At the beginning of the twentieth century, neither environment as an integrative ecological concept nor the biosphere as the planetary life-support system was an object of international concern."

The post-war decades (1945–75) witnessed sharpened public concern about environmental pollution, especially in the industrialised countries. Rachel Carson's *Silent Spring* (1962) was, as Nicholson (1972) described it:

> "Probably the greatest and most effective single contribution hitherto towards informing public opinion on the nature and significance of ecology."

These decades also witnessed the birth and development of organised science programmes that concerned the entire planet. UNESCO, WMO, ICSU and IUCN share the credit for this initiation. Of direct bearing on global environmental issues were the International Geophysical year: (IGY) (1957–58) and the International Biological Programme: (IBP) (1964–1968).

As it progressed, the IBP helped us to understand the dynamics of eco-system as they function in their pristine condition and as manipulated by Man, the ecological processes of various biomes, and the interaction between humankind and the biosphere. Our undoing of the man-environment partnership and our awarness and appreciation of the threats and prospects of this relationship rested on measured information. The year 1968 seemed to mark a turning point. It led to what Nicholson (1983) described as "Our suddenly deepened and illuminated perception of our relation to Planet Earth and its natural resources."

Four significant events took place in 1968:

1. Responding to an initiative led by the Swedish Government, the United Nations General Assembly decided to convene the UN Conference on the Human Environment (Stockholm, 1972). The preparatory process for this conference (1969–1972) was a world-wide campaign for environmental awareness;
2. UNESCO held its intergovernmental conference on the biosphere, which was followed in 1969 by a symposium of experts to help outline what became UNESCO's "Man and the Biosphere (MAB) Programme," launched in 1971;
3. ICSU decided to establish its Scientific Committee on Problems of the Environment (SCOPE) which was to become an active organ of international ecological research and environmental studies;
4. A group of world citizens concerned about the future of humankind formed, under the leadership of the late Aurelio Peccei, the Club of Rome, which was to become instrumental in initiating studies on global resources and development, and debates on worldwide problems.

These paved the way for the 1970s which witnessed a series of UN conferences on: human environment (1972), population (1974), human settlements (1976), water (1977), desertification (1977), and the establishment of the United Nations Environmental issues became prominent in national concerns and in regional and international collaborative programmes.

During the 1980s, environmental issues gained prominence on the political agendas of national, regional and international action. Problems of the transboundary movement of pollutants led to regional action programmes and international agreements. UNEP initiated programmes covering ten marine bodies amenable to regional collaborative action for protecting the environment and conserving its resources. An international convention (1985) and associated protocol (1987) for the protection of the stratosphere ozone became the first management tool for a global environmental problem. A convention on the international movement of hazardous wastes was adopted in 1989. Consultations regarding agreements on other global problems (climate biodiversity etc.) are in progress.

Now, the concept of environmentally sound and sustainable development clearly implies not only protection of the environment and the rational use of resources but also a whole series of policy options in the economic, social and cultural sphere—not least, a commitment to equity and the eradication of poverty. This calls for close policy cooperation and commitment at the highest levels, making the role of UN family crucial in the implementation of the corresponding part of Agenda 21. Besides, effective action also requires an effective link between substantive activities and financial support and this in turn necessitates closer cooperation and information exchange between the UN system and other relevant GOs and NGOs as well as multilateral funding organisations.

Environmental standards and values are a concern not only of the scientists and planners but also of lawyers and legislators. The legal machinery with which standards are to be enforced is a significant part of the regime of pollution control. Without law, environmental standards cannot be enforced; without law, violation of standards cannot be effectively met.

Initially, the Constitution of India did not make any specific provisions to deal with environmental pollution. However, as an indirect reference Article 47 may be referred to. It was in the year 1976 that by the 42nd amendment two-fold provisions were added in the Constitution. On the one hand, it directed the State for the protection and improvement of environment and, on the other, it cast a duty on every citizen to help in the preservation of natural environment. For the protection and improvement of environment, it is enjoined on the State that the State shall endeavour to protect and improve the environment and to safeguard the forests and wildlife of the country.[1] Similarly, it is one of the fundamental duties of every citizen of India to protect and improve the natural environment including forests, lakes, rivers and wildlife, and to have compassion for living creatures.[2]

Public Interest Litigation, which according to Krishna Iyer J., is the new jurisprudence of constitutional law has played a creative and constructive role in the field of environmental protection. The same can be evident from Chapter III & V.

In a developing country with uneducated masses, conditions of abject poverty, where the awareness of socio-economic and ecological problems is alarmingly lacking, the judiciary must come forward actively to make good the deficiency and meet *inter alia* the challenges of the problems of pollution. Besides the traditional function of interpretation and application of the law, the judiciary can perform the educative function of bringing an awarness of the massive problems of pollution, through a series of illuminating judgements. If one goes through Chapter V, he will be satisfied that the judiciary has done much more than was expected.

Chapter IV deals with Forest and Wildlife. The historical background of the forest laws alongwith the judicial pronoucement have been discussed in detail. The Wildlife (Protection) Act, 1972 alongwith the different projects and sanctuary etc. have been dealt with in detail.

The last chapter i.e. Chapter VI of the book is with regard to 'Environmental Education'. In view of the importance of this chapter, suggestions for the development of the curriculum at different levels have been given.

A conclusion at the end projects the need for a simultaneous approach for environmental protection and development.

REFERENCES

1. Article 48A of the Constitution of India.
2. Article 51A(g) *ibid.*

CHAPTER I

ENVIRONMENTAL CHANGE AND SCIENCE AND TECHNOLOGY INSTITUTIONS

Global Perspective

Environmental issues, during the recent times have become world-wide concern. Until now, however, the R & D effort to deal with them has been modest in most countries. This is due, in part, to inertia inherent in related organisations as well as in broad economic and social contexts. On the other hand, newly recognised changes of a global nature, endangering the future of the planet as whole, raise even more complex questions for science and technology institutions and programmes.[1]

In the present century, environmental degradation has emerged as a major global concern for human survival. A large number of international and global organisations with the collective wisdom of scientists, economists and planners have come up to settle the environmental issues confronting the nations and the physical world. The environmental crisis has convinced the world to use technology and resources to repair the damage already done to our environment and also to patent substitutes for certain harmful chemicals in order to protect and preserve nature and natural resources.[2]

We cannot ignore the fact that what causes many of the environmental effects will always remain uncertain as most studies of the greenhouse effect and that of climate change cannot be tested conclusively. In next quarter century period, more people will die from road accidents, AIDS, earthquakes/floods and smoking cigarettes than from the hole in the Ozone layer. Perhaps the Sahel drought cause the destruction of Amazon and the disastrous flood in Bangladesh is the impact of global warming on the climate. But it is questionable whether starvation is caused by deforestation or drowning or coal burning on the other side of the world.

Official public perception of environmental challenges has moved through three[4] broad phases, such as (1) through the early seventies, (2) from the mid-seventies to the mid-eighties, (3) since the mid-eighties.

(1) Through the Early Seventies

Prior to the late 1960s, the environment received little attention, and what are now viewed as environment challenges were seen as specific problems. In most OECD (Organisation for Economic Co-operation and Development), they principally involved threats to the quality of air and water and, in response, elicited *ad hoc* legislative and regulatory reactions, generally of a local nature.

From the late 1960s onwards, clearer notions of the environment and a sense of the need to protect it grew among most OECD countries. In particular, increasing fears about natural resource depletion reflected in the "Club of Rome" activities.[5] More generally, the Stockholm Conference (1972) reflected these growing environmental concerns and gave impetus to institutionalisation. Special departments and agencies were established in the early 1970s in a number of countries, including France, Germany, Norway, Sweden, the United Kingdom, and the United States, with both regulatory and promotional responsibilities. An OECD Committee for Environment was established in 1970. All these developments marked the beginning of the recognition that environmental problems were not simply *ad hoc* pollution problems.

(2) From the Mid-seventies to the Mid-eighties

The elaboration of more coherent views was partially side-tracked during the late 1970s by successive energy crises of 1974 and 1979, and associated macro-economic developments. In retrospect, the energy-driven development can be seen to have yielded important environmental benefits: fossil-fuel energy use has been recognised as the biggest single source of pollution, and, as a result, the pre-occupation with energy efficiency which grew out of these crises has led to the considerable increase in energy efficiency—for example, in terms of energy use per $ of GDP—that have been realised since 1973,[5] and at the same time, the macro economic and political attention and, perhaps, the evolution of environmental thinking from other objectives.

(3) Since the Mid-eighties

Since the middle 1980s, renewed attention to the environment and a great increase in policy activities can be observed. However, both scope and focus of environmental concerns have evolved considerably. Three[6] emerging areas of preoccupation can be identified: *the volume of pollutants, the nature of pollution* and *the geographical focus*.

(i) A massive increase in the volume of pollutants has been associated with sustained rapid GDP growth and especially with the exponential growth in the use of fossil fuels: to some extent, these trends are already being checked within the OECD countries, where the rate of growth of fossil fuel use per capita is now falling, but the legacy of the earlier growth is still apparent, especially in relation to global climate change.

(ii) As regards the nature of pollution, micro-toxicity has been spreading, as the product of advances in chemical (and more recently, nuclear) technology during this century; some products are proving both highly toxic and very long-lived, e.g. chlorofluorocarbons (CFCs), although it should be recognised that micro-toxins, including radioactive materials, are not all man-made.

(iii) There has been shift in geographical focus from problems primarily located in OECD countries to those of central and eastern European and developing countries, and a parallel shift from the local to the regional and, most recently, to the global level.

Moreover, environmental thinking is moving towards the notions of 'sustainable development' defined by the World Commission of Environment and Development in the Bruntland Report.[6] Essentially these notions shift attention from degradation of the physical environment towards the conditions under which the geosphere/biosphere can sustain long-term equitable development for the welfare of all its people.

The recent shifts in the perception of environmental threats have had several consequences for policy makers and for the S & T community. *First,* the focus has been shifted to some extent from immediate to long term problems. *Second*, some risks are now perceived as far more serious than what had been previously thought. *Finally* and perhaps most importantly, the relative lack of sufficient documentation leads to great uncertainty. As a result, the S & T community is increasingly asked to make diagnosis and suggest solutions to problems at the limit of current knowledge, while policy makers must increasingly devise policies in situations of massive uncertainty.

(a) Global Climate Problems

Global climate problems appear to be emerging. One concerns with the ozone depletion detected in the stratosphere over the Antarctic and perhaps, now the Atlantic and the other involves global warming (the "green house effect"). The two problems are seen, to a certain extent, as separate. There may be lessons to be drawn from the differing involvement of the S & T community in the policy process.[7]

(b) Ozone Depletion

Ozone depletion results in greater ultra-violet radiation reaching the earth. Effects include greater incidence of (skin) cancers and, possibly, more important effects on the ecology of flora and fauna in high latitudes. In terms of S & T policy, diagnosis of the emerging problem was swift and effective, beginning with reports in the early 1980s. Governments and industry also responded swiftly, with a commitment (the Montreal Protocol) to phase out CFC's during the 1990s. Implementation is yet to take full effect but is more or less assured in the OECD countries. Some 65 per cent of 1985 global CFC emissions came from OECD countries and only 18 per cent from developing countries. However, the share of the latter could rise to 45 per cent by the year 2000.[8]

The implications of implementation of technology development and industrial structures remain uncertain. CFC's are primarily used in refrigeration and air-conditioning, in insulating materials and in the cleaning of electronic components. Globally, the most challenging difficulty is to replace CFC's in refrigeration and air-conditioning, because the resulting user cost increase imply "sustainable development" trade-offs in terms of health, especially in developing countries. In addition, only a very small number of firms possess CFC production technology and are capable of producing substitutes. In global terms, countries that use CFCs but do not possess the relevant technologies are important polluters, and it is not clear how far normal market mechanisms will incite them to adopt non-polluting alternatives.[9]

(c) Global Warming

Global warming by "greenhouse gas" is a more intractable policy problem. It concerns man-made emissions of carbon dioxide (CO_2) and several other gases—essentially, CFCs, methane and nitrous oxide—associated with agriculture and fossil fuel combustion. Given that agricultural emissions are increasingly a non-OECD concern and that CFCs are being phased out, most of the OECD countries' science and policy efforts with respect to the carbon cycle are of high priority. It would be remembered that apart from global warming, CO_2 is not a pollutant, it is a product of most natural activities and, especially, of combustion of fossil fuels.[10]

Perception of global warming threats is very recent. The existence of long term variations in global average temperatures has long been established, but it is now feared that we face relatively short term shifts in temperature due to man-made activities during this century, and specially in the past few decades. In 1988, the Inter-governmental Panel on Climate Change (IPCC) was established by the World Meteorology Organisation (WMO) and the United Nations Environment Programme (UNEP) to investigate the problem. Some 200 climatologists were involved and altogether about 400 scientists were consulted. The IPCC exercise undoubtedly produced the largest international consultation of scientists on an identifiable set of problems to date. The findings of its three Working Groups (June 1990) reflect a considerable effort to draw usable consensus, conclusions from many disparate research activities. There has, inevitably, been some subsequent criticism from scientists whose views were not included or who point to disparities between the working groups, and, to a small extent, from those who feel that the panelists form a self interested lobby to justify further research. However, most observers and most OECD governments judge that the IPCC findings furnish the best present overall assessment and provide the basis for policy discussion and further research. The IPCC conclusions are appended below:

> The IPCC estimates that, with continuation of present policies, global mean temperatures will rise by about 0.3 degree celsius per decade and lift average temperatures from present levels by 1 degree by 2025 and three degrees by the end of next century. With somewhat less confidence, the IPCC judges that this will lead to global mean sea-level rise of about 6 cm per decade. These rates of predicted change are much greater than those experienced in previous climate changes. However, the pace of global climate change remains uncertain, because of potential offsetting and delaying phenomena. In particular, there is great uncertainty about effects on cloud formation, on the role of oceans in absorbing heat and CO_2 and on developments in Antarctic (and, perhaps, Arctic) ice masses. Finally, with much less confidence, IPCC judges that the impact on balance will be negative, for tens of millions of people

living on low-lying lands, for agriculture in vulnerable areas and, perhaps, for international trade in basic food products.[11]

Governments, at a meeting in Geneva, in November, 1990, largely accepted these findings and a number of them have committed themselves to considerable reductions in CO_2 emissions. Nevertheless, since decisions to reduce fossil fuel energy use have important macro economic implications, there is considerable policy hesitation on the means of attaining the desired levels.[12]

Important reduction in greenhouse gases emissions can be achieved through adoption of present "best practice" energy technologies (essentially by bringing North America, developing countries and central and Eastern Europe into line with Western Europe and Japan). This does not require technological innovation, but could imply structural shifts in industry and in consumer product demand. Less energy intensive technologies and, within the energy sector, technologies that produce less CO_2 (hydro, nuclear and solar) could be developed. In the longer term, it may be possible to tackle the carbon cycle and remove CO_2 from the atmosphere.[13]

In S & T terms, these responses are different and competing and thus simply difficult policy decisions. It is important to stress the uncertainty surrounding prospective global climate developments. The highest S & T priority must therefore be better understanding of the processes involved, including R & D for earth-observing instruments (e.g. satellites). Beyond this, most scientists advocate the "precautionary principle": we should minimise irreversible changes in global and local ecosystems, notably by reducing fossil fuel energy. It is certain that global warming is occurring. It is prudent to begin research to meet the challenge, although none of the adverse effects is likely to have significant impact for some 20 years.[14]

At the international level mention may be made of the establishment of the International Group of Funding Agencies for Global Change Research, set up under the auspices of ICSU, at the initiative of NSF. The United States has launched an important inter-agency programme ($US 1 billion of spending planned in FY 1991 Budget). Japan has recently established an "Institute of Industrial Technology for the Global Environment", notably with a view to undertake R & D on removal of CO_2 from the atmosphere.[15]

National Perspective

(a) General

The environmental movement in India, which for all purposes, had its beginning in the year, 1972, the year of the Stockholm Conference,[15A] is by now more than twenty years old. In India, potential sources on pollution are found in energy chemicals, additives, fertilisers, synthetic fibers, metallurgy, ceramic industries, pharmaceutical industry, sulphuric and nitric acid producing industry, domestic consumption of low-grade fuels, use of automobiles, garbage and solid waste.

The screaming caravan of transport carriers, travelling through cities and towns, blenching black smoke from the diesel engines is a common sight in our country. The increased use of auto-rickshaws, buses, lorries, truck and treckers carrying with them an increased air pollution potential which has a telling effect on the urban population's health.

In last two decades the urban population in India has nearly doubled, from 109.5 million in 1971 to 217.0 million in 1991 and it is expected to reach 325 million by the turn of the century. With the increase urbanisation along with the conglomeration of industries and commercial activities in the urban areas, the transport demand has also consequently increased. Due to an inadequate public transport system, the use of personalised vehicles has been steadily increasing. The total number of vehicles has been steadily increasing. The total number of vehicles in India has increased from about 11 million in 1986 to more than 21 million in 1991. About one fifth of the vehicular population in India is concentrated in the major metropolitan cities.[16]

(b) Two-wheeler Predominance

Another distinctive feature of vehicular population in India is the fact that nearly 70 per cent of the vechiles are two- and three-wheelers which are mostly two-stroke engine driven, while petrol driven vehicles with four-stroke engines constitute only 14 per cent and the diesel driven vehicles make up 8 per cent of the total. Evidently, two-wheelers are becoming the most popular mode of vehicular transport. The number of two-wheelers has been growing at a rate of about 20 per cent a year and it is estimated that these vehicles will be around 36 million by the turn of the century as against 7 million in 1987. It is expected that passenger car and diesel vehicles will double by that time. While two-wheelers are preferred for personal transport, three-wheelers (auto-rickshaws) serve as an important mode of intermediate public transport. The two- and three-wheelers are likely to constitute 80 per cent of the vehicles in 2000 A.D. and most of these will operate in the urban areas.[17]

The consumption of gasoline and diesel by the road transport sector has increased from 1.5 and 7.2 million tonnes—which is approximately one per cent of world fuel consumption.[18]

Compared to several European countries and the U.S., the vehicular population in India is still relatively low. But, even with this modest population, vehicular pollution has become a serious problem in the urban area. Apart from the concentration of vehicles in the urban area, the other factors are the types of engines used, age of vehicles, congested traffic, poor road conditions and outdated automotive technologies.[19]

More than 1.8 million vehicles ply every day in Delhi. The automobiles are responsible for 60 per cent of the air pollution in the capital city. In a case with regard to vehicular pollution in Delhi, the Supreme Court came to the rescue of helpless public exposed to the grave dangers and health hazards created by the emission of the vehicles.

For prevention and control of vehicular pollution, it is necessary to have a multi-pronged approach. This should, *inter-alia,* be addressed to the following tasks:

1. Upgradation of fuel quality and use of cleaner fuel.
2. Reduction of lead content in motor-spirit.
3. Enforcement of emission standards for vehicles on the road at the manufacturing stage.
4. Public transport facilities.
5. Improvement of roads and traffic systems.
6. Zoning of areas for regulation of traffic movement.
7. Restriction on indiscriminate growth of urban centres, industrial and commercial activites.

Keeping in view, the above the efforts for reducing vehicular pollution are being made mainly in four directions such as (i) improvement and change in the engine, (ii) fuel, (iii) catalitic converter and (iv) silencing system.

The Delhi administration has not been able to have a grip over the problem of vehicular pollution inspite of many attempts.

A recent suvery reveals that "every day millions of gallons of trade wastes and effluents are discharged into the rivers, streams, lakes and sea etc." Indiscriminate water pollution is a problem all over the world but is now acute in densely populated industrial cities, India is no exception to this.[20]

Deforestation and denudation have converted many parts of the country from green to brown.

Pollution of the environment has many dimensions. Third world countries have problems of mass poverty. If one wants that pollution is controlled, then he has to do his best to eradicate poverty.

The reasons of environmental pollution in India are many. Night soil and garbage which cause pollution of the environment can be best utilised by converting it to manure and bio gas. In this regard a passage from the book written by Paul Harrison "The Third World Tomorrow" is quoted below:

> "The potential of bio gas is considerable. If all the dung of India's live stock, and all human wastes, were fermented, this would meet the domestic fuel requirements of three out of four families and the savings in manure of fuel could be worth one billion dollar a year or more. Other countries are now realising the importance of bio gas. China which does not have India's cultural and social obstacles, use bio gas widely; in 1977 around 5 million plants are in use."

Talking about global threat to environment from man-made chemicals, one cannot ignore the fact that a handful of industrialised nations produce 80% of these so called environment damaging chemical substances. While 20% is spread out globally in other developing countries. Thus, the stringent measures applicable for these developed nations may not be necessary to be the same for developing countries. How relevant are these issues in the economic, ecological status of individual nations and regions should be examined and understood first. Thus, any effort to globalise these issues without establishing evidence of ill effects, may only harm the process of industralisation in developing world.[21]

Instead of joining hands with the outcry of developed nations on environmental issues, developing countries like India will be better off, if we focus our attention to the following:[22]

- Ensure clean and hygenic living and working conditions for the people;
- Sponsor research on environment issues pertaining to the region;
- Ensure safety against known and proven industrial hazards;
- Find economical methods for salvaging hazardous industrial wastes;

- Encourage afforestation;
- Find out substitutes for proven hazardous materials based on local resources and needs instead of blindly depending on advanced nations to find solutions;
- Ensuring environmental education a part of school and college curriculum;
- Dissemination of authentic information to the masses concerning environment instead of making it an issue for journalistic over-reaction;
- Stop harassment of people and project proposals in the name of environmental protection. In other words, stop building up an elite environmental lobby instead make it known to everyone that environment belongs to all and equally and it is a common public education, information and participation, without which nothing can be achieved.

We must address ourselves for framing sensible environment policies based on our own resources and technology. There is also no coherent national policy on environment on thrust areas. Nor there is any organised effort to address growing shortage of trained scientists, engineers and professionals in the area of environment. It is submitted, let us first get on with the basics instead of getting trapped into controversies.[23]

REFERENCES

1. Science and Technology Policy, Review and Outlook, 1991, Organisation for Economic Co-oparation and Development.
2. Chatterjee Anjana, *Need for Fresh Thinking on Environmental Issues*, Yojna, June 1–15 (1990) p. 23.
3. *Ibid.*
4. Report of the Regional Conference on the World Commission on Environment and Development (WCED) in the ECE region, Bergen, 8–16 May, 1990.
5. *Sustainable Development, Science and Policy*, NAVP Norwegian Research Council for Science and the Humanities, Sandakerveien 99, 0483 Oslo 4.
6. A conference organised by the Norwegian Research Council for Science and the Humanities, in liaison with the European Science Foundation, and in co-operation with the Regional Conference on the Report of the World Commission on Environment and Development (WCED) in ECE region, Bergen, 8–16 May, 1990.
7. *Infra* note 5 pp. 54–55.
8. *Ibid.*
9. *Ibid.*
10. The World of Environment: Two Decades of Challenge, edited by Mostafa K. Tolba and other published by Chapman and Hall, London.
11. *Supra* note 1, p. 56.

12. *Ibid.*
13. *Ibid.*
14. *Ibid.*
15. *Ibid.*

15A. The Global concern for environmental protection found expression in the UN Conference on Human Environment held at Swedish capital Stockholm in June, 1972. The conference adopted an action plant relating to subject areas of human settlement and human health, territorial eco-system, environment and development, oceans, energy and natural disasters. It proposed institutional arrangements for implementing the action plan within the UN systems. The recommendations of the Action Plan were accepted under the UNEP. Subsequent conferences were held at Nairobi, Vienna, Montreal, New Delhi, Beijing, Kuala Lumpur and Rio.

16. *Vehicular Pollution*: *Combating the Smog and Noise in Cities*, The Hindu Survey of the Environment, 1994, p. 41.
17. *Ibid.*
18. *Ibid.*
19. *Ibid.*
20. Srivastav Suresh C., Water Pollution, Academy Law Review, pp. 137–138.
21. *Supra* note 2.
22. *Ibid.*
23. *Ibid.*

CHAPTER II

ENVIRONMENT AND THE CONSTITUTION OF INDIA

Introduction

The Constitution of India came into force on the 26th January 1950. At its initial stage there was no direct and specific provision with regard to environmental pollution. There was, however, an indirect reference to the subject of environment in Article 47 of the Constitution, reads as follows:

> "The State shall regard the raising of the level of nutrition and standard of living of its people and *improvement of public health*[1] as among its primary duties."

Of course, there is provision of "public health and sanitation" in entry 6 of State list.

The Constitution (forty-second Amendment) Act, 1976 has introduced several far reaching changes in the fundamental law of the country by inserting and emitting provisions in its different articles to make it adaptable to changing situations. In the light of Stockholm Declaration on Human environment, 1992, India, by the above amendment added new provisions to give it an environmental dimension.[2]

One of the significant amendment to the fundamental law relates to the protection of wildlife. Article 48(a) has been added to the chapter of Directive Principles of State Policy which states:

> "The State shall endeavour to protect and improve the environment and to safeguard the forest and wildlife of the country."

Relying upon the above provision of the Constitution, the Supreme Court of India in *M.C. Mehta (II)* v. *Union of India,* [3] gave directions to the Central and State Governments and various local bodies and Boards under the various statutes to take appropriate steps for the prevention and control of pollution of water.

There has been several instances where the rice wealth of the forest, has been considerably reduced by those who indulge in robing forest wealth for monetary gains. With the gradual extinction of forests, the existence of wildlife is also endangered, as the existence of forest is an indispensable requisite for the very existence of wildlife. They are so interdependent that one cannot exist without the other. Theft of forest wood, specially the sandal-wood and the hunting of wildlife for the purpose of trading of skin and other valuable parts of the animal body have been rather contrary to the national interest.

The fast industralisation and urbanisation has been another factor for deteriorating conditions of the forests and the wildlife. Large number of trees have been destroyed for construction of roads and buildings for giving a new urban look to the modern cities. It is also stated that such extinction of trees resulted in the failure of rains. As safeguarding the forest and wildlife has become important, the State should not undertake any activity, which may threaten the existence of forest and its eventual effect on the continuity of wildlife. Forest in India contain rich wealth and are unique in that they possess rare animal species. Further the Wildlife Act already enacted to protect the wildlife requires strict implementation. In view of this, Article 48A was inserted by forty-second Amendment Act, 1976.[4]

Purity of the air we breathe-in and the water we drink is absolutely essential for good health.[5] Equally important is the environment in which we live and work. In view of this, Article 51A (g) of the Constitution also introduced by 42nd Amendment lays down the following:

> "It shall be the duty of every citizen of India to protect and improve the natural environment including forests, lakes, rivers and wildlife and to have compassion for living creatures."

The above is one of the fundamental duties of every citizen of India. Fundamental duties have also been incorporated in some of the constitutions[6] in order to declare some of the basic duties of the individual with a view to inculcate in them the sense of responsibility to the community. A mere declaration of fundamental duties could have no legal sanction unless specific laws are enacted to enforce such duties. Specific laws have been enacted to control environmental pollution. These laws have been dealt within the next chapter.

Besides the provisions contained in Articles 47, 48 and 51A (g), there are some provisions in the Constitution in view of which environmental laws can be enacted by the Indian Parliament. Such provisions contain in Part-XI of the Constitution. For instance, as per Article 246(1) and (3) of the Constitution, Parliament can enact laws with respect to matters contained in the Union List of the Seventh Schedule and State Legislature with respect to matters contained in the State List. But as per Article 246(2), the Parliament and State Legislature of any State are competent to make any laws with respect to any of the matters contained in the concurrent list of the seventh schedule.[7] Parliament can also enact laws in respect of environmental protection under Articles 248, 252 and 253 of the Constitution.[8] Article 253 empowers the Parliament for exclusive legislation. In view of the Stockholm Conference and provision contained in Articles 248, 252 and 253, the Water (Prevention and Control of Pollution) Act, 1974 and the Air (Prevention and Control of Pollution) Act, 1981 were enacted. It appears that centre can enact legislations on environmental issues under the provisions contained in Articles 248, 252 and 253. But in reality it is not so. It is difficult to administer all Central enactment and therefore, Article 258 of the Constitution empowers the Union to confer powers on States in certain matters.[9]

Public Interest Litigation

Until quite recently the paradise of justice was the monopoly of the rich who could afford it. This class-oriented Common Law justice system is now giving way to the new pass-oriented jurisprudence. Access to justice through 'class action', 'public interest litigation' and 'representation proceedings' is the present constitutional jurisprudence, Krishan Iyer J. declared.[10]

In the recent past, public interest litigation has played a unique role in the fields like—protection of fundamental rights, human rights, consumer protection, social justice and environmental protection etc. The concept of Public Interest Litigation is comparatively of recent origin and is attributable to the modern trend of judicial activism and dynamic and unconventional approach by the courts to the problem that they are required to tackle. What had been in vogue in our judicial system was the rule of *locus standi* that a petition under Article 32 can only be considerabley relaxed by the Supreme Court. In *Ratlam Municipal Corporation* v. *Vercichand,*[11] Krishna Iyer J. recognising PIL as constitutional obligation of the court observed:

> "Social Justice is due to the people and therefore, the people must be able to trigger off the jurisdiction vested for their benefit in any public functionary. . . . In the exercise of such power, the judiciary must be informed by the broader principle of access to justice necessitated by the conditions of developing countries and obligate by Article 38 of the Constitution."

The above case is an example of the Supreme Court's effort to give effect to the constitutional imperatives. It proved the consciousness of the judiciary to a problem which had not attracted much attention upto that time. The Supreme Court responded with equal anxiety and raised the issue to come within the mandate of the Constitution. The case also reflected the spirit of Article 51A(g) of the Constitution that it is the duty of every citizen to protect and improve the environment.

The aforesaid case also set forth the path for the public interest litigation, a concept which is further articulated by the Supreme Court in number of pronouncements.[12]

In *S.P. Gupta* v. *Union of India,*[13] popularly known as the judges' transfer case, speaking for the majority, Bhagwati J. said:

> "Procedure being merely a hand maiden of justice, it should not stand in the way of access to justice to the weaker section of the Indian humanity and, therefore where the poor and disadvantaged are concerned. . . , this court will not insist on a regular writ petition and even a letter addressed by a public-spirited individual or a social action group acting *pro bono publico* would suffice to invite the jurisdiction of this court."

As a result of this broad view of *locus standi*, spate of environmental cases have been brought before the courts through public interest litigations. They have been filed either by individual, voluntary organisations or by letters/petitions sent to the judges.

Having been permitted by the court, public spirited persons have brought into limelight the grievances of others.[14]

In *Kinkri Devi* v. *Himachal Pradesh*;[15] the High Court delivered a significant judgement on environmental protection. In the instant case, a petition was filed by some concerned citizens in the High Court on the basis of an article published in a newspaper on the problem of quarrying in Paonta Sahib in Sirmur District of Himachal Pradesh, which resulted in the court's order to stop destruction of the hills.

In Articles 48A and 51A(g) there is both a constitutional pointer to the State and a constitutional duty of the citizens not only to protect but also to improve the environment and to preserve and safeguard the forests, the flora and fauna, the rivers and lakes and all the other water resources of the country. To ensure the attainment of the constitutional goal of the protection and improvement of the natural wealth and environment and of the safeguarding of the forests, the lakes, the rivers and the wildlife and to protect the people inhabiting the vulnerable areas from the hazardous consequences of the arbitrary exercise of the power of granting mining leases and of indiscriminate operation of the mines on the strength of such leases without due regard to their life, liberty and property, the court will be left with no alternative but to intervene effectively by issuing appropriate writs, orders and directions including the direction as to the closure of the mines, the operation whereof is proving to be hazardous and the total prohibition of the grant or renewal of mining leases till the Government evolves a long term plan based on a scientific study with a view to regulating the exploitation of the minerals in the State without detriment to the environment, the ecology, the natural wealth and resources and the local population. However, the need for judicial intervention may not arise even in those cases where the court's jurisdiction is invoked, if the administration takes preventive, remedial and curative measures meanwhile.[16]

In view of Article 51A(g) of the Constitution, preservation of the environment and keeping the ecological balance unaffected is a task which not only government but also every citizen must undertake. The Public Interest Litigation has now made the discharge of this duty for the public easier. In the year 1983, a case of this type came when a letter written by Rural Litigation and Entitlement Kendra, Dehradun to the apex court was treated as a writ petition.[17] The fact of the case was in Doon Valley, the mine owners and lessees were carrying on erratic irrational and uncontrolled quarrying of limestone. Mining operation had led to cutting down of the forests resulting in stripping the landscape base of its verdant cover. Digging of limestone and allowing the waste to roll down or carried down by rain water to the lower levels had affected the villages and the agricultural lands located below the hills. The naturally formed streams had been blocked. Blasting had disturbed the natural calm. It had loosened the rocky structure by shaking the soil, thereby disturbing the entire ecology of the area. There was growing apprehension that if the mining was carried on in unrestricted manner, a stage would come when there would be dearth of water in the entire belt.

The Supreme Court immediately made an order directing all fresh quarrying to be stopped and called upon the District Magistrate and Superintendent of Police of Dehra Dhun District to strictly enforce that order. Later the Court, after hearing the counsel for parties, appointed a committee to inspect and determine whether there was a danger of landslides and if there was any other hazard to individuals, cattle or agricultural lands by reason of the carrying of mining operations.

The Court by its order of March, 1985[18] directed the closure of certain lime stone quarries on the ground that there were serious deficiencies regarding safety and hazards in them. Expressing its concern on the maintaining of the ecological balance the court observed:[19]

> "Preservation of environment and keeping the ecological balance unaffected is a task which not only government but also every citizen must undertake. It is a social obligation and every citizen is reminded that it is his fundamental duty as enshrined in Article 51A(g) of the Constitution . . . . Governments—both at the Centre and in the States must realise and remain cognigant of the fact that the stake involved in the matter is large and far-reaching. The civil consequences would last long. Once that unwanted situation sets in, amends or repairs would no be possible. The greenery of India, as some doubt, may perish and the Thar desert may expand its limit."

Further, the court pointed out that it is always to be remembered that these are permanent assets of mankind and are not intended to be exhausted in one generation as such tapping of resources have to be done with requisite attention and care so that ecology and environment may not be affected in any serious way. Planning must be undertaken to preserve national wealth.

The Supreme Court's judgement in Rural Litigation and Entitlement Kendra[20] is a pace-setter and goes a long way in the people's campaign of environmental protection. The case also makes the people and government—both at the Union and the States, conscious of their constitutional obligation and makes the life of the people comfortable and live in an unpolluted environment.

Janik v. *Sardarnagar Municipality*[21] is another significant case with regard to public interest litigation relating to environmental protection. In this case a letter written by two persons living in Chharanagar on the outskirts of Ahmadabad city was directed to be treated as a petition by the downtrodden section of the society. Their repeated complaints about the dirty and unhygenic surroundings was never heeded to. During rainy season, the entire area was submerged with water as there was no provision of outletting the dirty water.

The Gujarat High Court gave a direction to the State Government as well as to the Municipal authorities to immediately work out a scheme to provide permanent sewerage and drainage system. Action was taken accordingly. The court observed:[22]

> "The court places on record its appreciation of the attitude of the Government in this case in co-operating with the Sardarnagar Municipality to extend the much needed relief to the residents of Chharanagar area. A litigation started in the interests of such residents by a petition by two of the residents addressed to this Court has achieved the result by reason of the Sardarnagar Municipality and the State Government adopting reasonable postures."

Introduction of New Procedures and Techniques in PIL

In no time PIL became very popular and it started crowding the courts—sometimes in the form of letters and sometimes as skimpy petitions based on newspaper reports. All these led the judges to evolve new procedures and techniques to facilitate this new type of litigation. Broadly speaking, judicial innovation was required to adopt the following procedures;

(i) secure detailed facts, since the petitioner's information was usually sketchy;
(ii) receive expert testimony in cases involving complex social and scientific issues; and
(iii) ensure the continuous supervision of prospective judicial order.

To construct a complete framework of the facts, a judge often requires the concerned public officials to furnish detailed, comprehensive affidavits. Sometimes, where a swift, impartial assessment of the facts is needed and the official machinery is unreliable, slow or biased, an affidavit may be helpful. In such cases, the courts appoint special commissions to gather facts and data. The power to appoint commission is an inherent power of the Supreme Court under Article 32 of the Constitution and the High Courts under Article 226.[22A]

The Commissioner is a responsible person and hence his report is always treated as *prima facie* evidence of the facts and data gathered. After the report is received by the court, copies of the same are supplied to the parties, who may choose to dispute the contents of the report in an affidavit. The court then considers the report in light of the affidavits and proceeds to decide the issues involved.

In *L.K. Koolwal* v. *State of Rajasthan*.[22B] the petitioner prayed for direction to the municipal authority of Jaipur to solve the city's acute sanitation problems. The Rajasthan High Court appointed a commissioner to report on the insanitary conditions in various parts of the city. Here the commissioner discharged the task assigned to him to the satisfaction of the Court. In *Sergio Carvalho* v. *State of Goa*,[22C] however, the Bombay High Court's experience with a commissioner was less sanguine. The petitioner challenged the development permission for a beach resort on the Goa coast. Since work at the beach site had commenced, the Court appointed a commissioner to inspect and report on the extent of the construction. In this report the commissioner went beyond his fact-finding task of describing the development on the beach and commented on the legality of the structures. The High Court criticised the commissioner for exceeding his brief, and rejected the subjective portions of the report.

The third technique adopted by the courts to ease the environment petition's evidentiary burden, is the resort to judicial notice of the "facts". For example, in *M.C. Mehta* v. *Union of India*,[22D] a petition seeking to reduce pollution of the river Ganga, the Supreme Court dispensed with the need for hard scientific proof on the health-effects of the pollution, the damage is caused to riparian property, and the manner in which it harmed the livelihood of those living downstream. In view of certain books and writings brought to the Court's notice, the judge simply assumed that such injuries either had occurred or were likely to occur, and proceeded to issue remedial directions.

Similarly, the Bombay High Court in another case[22E] took judicial notice of the poor state of the city's roads after the on-set of the monsoon. In the instant case, the secretary of a Taxi Drivers' Union and a newspaper editor made a petition to the court for compelling the Municipal Corporation's authorities to maintain the roads and keep it in good condition. The court appointed a committee agreed to the recommendations. The Municipal Corporation agreed to the recommendations submitted by the expert-committee and accordingly the petition was withdrawn.

In *Shriram Gas Leak Case*,[22F] it has been held by the apex court that independent scientific expertise is essential to inform judicial decision-making in environmental cases. In such cases, the court usually appoint a committee of experts to probe scientific questions and advise the court on a course of action. The expert committees, like the special commissions, are appointed under inherent powers of the Supreme Court and the High Courts under Articles 32 and 226 of the Constitution respectively. As the committee is consisted of eminent scientists drawn from dignified institutions, the court treats their opinion with great deference.

In *Shivarao Shantaram Wagle* v. *Union of India*,[22G] popularly known as Irish Butter Case, allegations were made that imported Irish butter targeted for distribution in Bombay was contaminated by the unclear fallout from the Chernobyl disaster, the Supreme Court appointed an expert committee to determine whether the imported milk and dairy products were safe for human consumption. When the committee reported that the milk products were safe, the Court released the butter for distribution.

Besides the above, there are some other cases such as, *Shriram Gas Leak Case*[22H] and *Dehradun Quarrying case*[22I] where the apex court has taken the help of the expert committee to dispose the matter. In the former case, the Supreme Court solicited the help of several expert committees. For instance, the Nilay Chaudhury Committee was appointed to advise the court on whether Shriram's hazardous chemical plant, which was located in Delhi, should be allowed to recommence operation in view of the danger to the neighbourhood. The committee was also asked to suggest measures to reduce the environmental threat that the plant posed. In the latter case the apex court enlisted an expert committee to evaluate the environmental impact of limestone quarrying operations in the Mussorie-Dehradun region. It is to be marked that the court also used the committee's mechanism for another purpose such as, to supervise the implementation of judicial orders. After this, a "Monitoring Committee" was formed to oversee the running of three limestone mines that had been allowed to continue operations, and to moniter reforestation measures in the region. Not only this but also a "Rehabilitation Committee" was formed to rehabilitate the mine oweners whose mines had been closed by the Court without payment of compensation.

Constitutional Interpretation with Regard to Environmental Protection

There is a marked difference between Articles 48A and 51A(g). In the former Article the expression 'environment' has been used whereas in the latter Article the expression 'natural environment' has been used. The difference is in form and not in substance. There is no dispute that

Part IV of the Constitution (Directive Principles) is non-justiciable but according to the constitutional provision,[23] no law giving effect to the policy of the State towards securing the principles specified in clause (b) or clause (c) of Article 39[24] of the Constitution shall be deemed to be void on the ground that it is inconsistent with, or takes away or abridges, any of the fundamental rights conferred by Article 14 of the Constitution which is on equality before law or Article 19 on protection of certain rights to freedom.

Therefore, it is clear that environmental legislation, designs to realise the objectives of Article 39, is immune from attack on the ground of conflict with some fundamental rights which are enshrined in part III of the Constitution and thus, is justiciable.

From the above discussion, it is clear that the constitutional provisions contain adequate safeguards for environmental protection and the recent concept of Public Interest Ligigation has made the task of the people for redressal of their grievances easier. Not only this, but also the Governments—Union an well as States and the people are duty bound to protect and improve the environment.

REFERENCES

1. The world *improvement of public health* imply a pollution free environment.
2. The Global concern for environment protection found expression in the UN Conference on Human Environment held at Swedish Captial Stockholm in June, 1992. The conference adopted an action plan relating to subject areas of human settlement and human health, territorial eco-systems, environment and development, oceans, energy and natural disasters. It proposed institutional arrangements for implementing the action plan were accepted under the UNEP. Subsequent conferences were held at Nairobi, Vienna, Montreal, New Delhi, Beijing, Kuala Lumpur and Rio.
3. (1988) I SCC 471 and AIR, 1988 SC.
4. Article 48A contained Section 10 of the Constitution (Forty-second Amendment) Act, 1976. It came into effect from 3rd January, 1977.
5. Today's industrial and urban society with its components like speedy transport, modern food processing, craving for miracle drugs, mechanised agriculture and desire for material prosperity and stability contribute to policy either directly or indirectly. It is medically proved that air pollution increases the incident of Emphyosemen, Bronchitis, Pneumonia and Asthama. It is suspected that air pollution is an ancillary cause of lung cancer, arteriosclerosis. It obscures vision, too.
6. Articles 59–68 of the Constitution of USSR 1977 (no broken); Article 1 of the Universal Declaration of Human Rights, 1948.
7. In fact the Constitution (Forty-second Amendment) Act, 1976 added the entries 17A, 17B and 20A on 'forests' (protection of wild animals and birds' and 'population control and family planning' respectively to the concurrent list, the former two of which figured earlier in the State List.

8. Article 253 Notwithstanding any thing in the forgoing provisions of this chapter, Parliament has power to make any law for the whole or any part of the territory of India for implementing any treaty, agreement or convention with any other country or countries or any decision made at any international conference, association or other body.

9. Article 258 (1) Notwithstanding anything in this Constitution, the President may with the consent of the Government of a State, entrust either conditionally or unconditionally to the Government or its officers functions in relation to any matter to which the executive power of the union extends.

(2) A law made by Parliament which applies in any State may, not withstanding that it relates to a matter with respect to which the Legislature of the State has no power to make laws, confer power and impose duties, upon the State or officers and authorities thereof.

(3) Where by virtue of this article, powers and duties have been conferred or imposed upon a State or officers or authorities thereof, there shall be paid by Government of India to the State such sum as may be agreed, or in default of agreement, as may be determined by any arbitrator appointed by Chief Justice of India, in respect of any extra costs of administration incurred by the State in Connection with the exercise of those powers and duties.

10. *ABSK Sangh (Rly)* v. *Union of India*, AIR, 1981 SC 298.
11. (1980) 4 SCC 162.
12. See *Dr. Upendra Buxi* v. *State of UP* (1981) 3 Scale 1136 and S.P. Gupta v. Union of India, AIR, 1982 SC.
13. *Supra* note 9 second.
14. In ABSK Sangh (Rly)'s case (*supra* note 10) it was held that the ABSK Sangh (Rly), though an unregistered association could maintain a writ petition under Article 32 for the redressal of a common grievance. Access to justice through 'class action', 'public interest litigation' and 'representative proceedings' is the present constitutional jurisprudence, declared Krishna Iyer J. See also the case which has been filed against the serious ground water contamination and environmental degradation caused by chemical industries near Bichari (Udaipur, Rajasthan) by the Indian Council for Enviro-legal. Action (ICELA), a voluntary organisation.
15. AIR, 1988 HP 04.
16. AIR, 1985 SC 652 and AIR 1887 SC 359.
17. *Rural Litigation and Entitlement Kendra* v. *State of UP*, AIR, 1985, SC 652.
18. *Ibid.*
19. *Ibid*, AIR 1987 SC 359 at 373.
20. *Supra* note 18 and 19.
21. AIR 1986, Guj. 49.
22. *Ibid.*
22A. *Bandhua Mukti Morcha* v. *Union & India*: AIR, 1984 SC 802.
22B. AIR 1988, Raj. 2.
22C. Writ Petition No. 367 of 1988.
22D. *Ganga Pollution (Tanneries) Case*, AIR, 1987 SC 965.

22E. *Anthony Lawrence Quadors* v. *Municipal Corporation of Greater Bombay*, writ petition No, 1129 of 1981 Bombay High Court, orders dated October 4, 1983 and April 11, 1985.

22F. *M.C. Mehta* v. *Union of India*, AIR 1987 SC 965.

22G. AIR 1988, SC 952.

22H. Supra note 22f.

22I. *Rural Litigation and Entitlement Kendra, Dehra Dun* v. *State of Uttar Pradesh* (Dehradun quarrying Case), AIR, 1987 SC 2187, 2195.

23. Article 31C of the Constitution of India.

24. Article 39 states as under:

"The State shall, in particular, direct its policy towards securing ...

(a) ...

(b) that the ownership and control of the material resources of the community are so distributed as best to subserve the common good;

(c) that the operation of the economic system does not result in the concentration of wealth and means or production.

CHAPTER III

ENVIRONMENTAL PROTECTION LEGISLATIONS

After going through the constitutional provisions regarding environmental protection, one is induced to ask about the specific laws relating to environmental protection.

Environmental laws are vast, undefined, exciting and glamourous. It is vast because of the various subjects and projects that lie within its ambit. It is mostly undefined in the sense of its rules. It is exciting in the newness of some of its techniques. It is glamourous in the publicity which it often receives.

The pre-world war II scenario in India betrays lack of governmental concern for environmental regulations in force during the colonial rules. Scattered provisions were to be found in certain statutes e.g., the Indian Penal Code, Criminal Procedure Code, the Prison Act, but their thrust was peripherial and limited to prevention of air and water pollution, preservation of forest and wild life. The Indian Penal Code penalised a person who voluntarily foul the water of any public spring or reservoir whereas the Factories Act required the owners to make effective arrangements for waste disposals. Similarly, the Fisheries Act imposed a penalty for killing of fish by poisoning the fauna and flora as well as wild life. However, the effect was piecemeal and fragmented and its implementation tardy.[1]

If we trace the history of the disastrous effect of environmental pollution as far back as 1348, we will find that the "Black Death" wiped 75 million people in Europe.[2] On the conclusion of the Second World war, the people of the world awoke to an uncertain dawn of a new era, uncertain because humanity was shocked by the miseries which the war had heaped upon it, particularly by the parting blow on Hiroshima, and a new era, because of its faith that it would, with the use of the new found technology, be able to build a better world by removing debris of the past.[3] And when we come down to the recent times, the saddest catastrophe of Bhopal resulted in the death of thousands of people and several lakhs were and are still suffering from the after effect of leakage of MIC and other toxic gases. This continued molestation of environment raised the eyebrows of legislatures at the national and international levels and laws were framed to control the present environmental pollution. In this case, the Indian legislature, fortunately, has not lagged behind and has shown great "concern for degradation of environment" and made "specific legislative attempts to control different pollutions and environmental pollution in particular."[4]

There are more than two hundred central and state legislations in India which directly or indirectly relate to environmental protection. The earliest being Shore Nuisance (Bombay and Colaba) Act, 1853 and the latest is the Environmental Protection Act, 1986.

Prior to 1974, the only recourse available to citizens against pollution of any nature was under the provision of the Indian Penal Code,[5] Criminal Procedure Code[6] and the Civil Procedure Code.[7] Suits claiming for tortuous liability were possible.[8] However, there were nothing in the nature of regulatory or preventive enactments as far as environmental pollution was concerned. All that the law provided for, was to proceed under civil or criminal law after the damage to environment took place.[9]

The procedural requirement of a regular civil court made relief very difficult. Very often, cases were lost on account of mere procedural and technical irregularities. It was only in the year 1974 that the Water (Prevention and Control of Pollution) Act 1974 was enacted. Then came the Water (Prevention and Control of Pollution) Cess Act, 1977 and the Air (Prevention and Control of Pollution) Act, 1981.[10]

Until 1981, the legislations with regard to environmental pollution were drawn up in piece-meal. Moreover, even these legislations were only punitive in nature and not preventive. Whatever little regulatory measures were provided for, in the laws, were never implemented. There was no clear demarcation of powers of the various authorities under the Acts and this often led to further confusions.[11]

The Environment (Protection) Act, 1986 was the first comprehensive legislation with regard to control of environmental pollution. It evoked encouraging response and support from all environmental groups. It was widely acclaimed as the first legislation with regard to control of environmental pollution. But the Act itself was a major disappointment as it was not very comprehensive in its scope and was not provided with sufficient powers to effectively bring to book offenders and control environmental pollution.[12]

The tables given below will, at a glance give an idea of legislations enacted by the Centre and States relating to control of environmental pollution. Different aspects of the Acts that are mentioned in the table, have been discussed in details separately.

In fact, India has among the finest bodies of environmental laws in the world. Among these: the Environmental Protection Act, 1986 (as well as the rules), the Water (Prevention and Control of Pollution) Act, 1974, the Water (Prevention and Control of Pollution) Cess Act, 1977, the Air (Prevention and Control of Pollution) Act, 1981 and the Forest (Conservation) Act, 1980.[12] To acquaint the readers, the above legislations have been discussed below in nutshell.

The Environmental Protection Act, 1986 (with rules)

(a) Definition

(i) Presence in the environment of any solid, liquid or gaseous substance in concentration so as to be injurious to environment.

(ii) Environment includes water, air and land and the inter-relationships which exist among and between water, air, land and human beings and other living creatures, plants, micro organisms and property.

(b) Objectives

Protection and improvement of the environment and matters connected therewith.

(c) Authorities

The Central Government constitutes the authority(ies) for the purpose of exercising powers and performing the function provided under the Act. The officers are appointed by the Central Government.

There is no separate official body at the State level.

The authorities under the Acts are essentially government officials. There is no involvement of people or environmental groups or activists in any of the authorities constituted under the various laws. As we shall subsequently see the scheme of the Act involves only around governmental agencies. There is much scope for active participation of citizens

Table I : A Selective List of Environment Related Central Enactments

General	Water Pollution	Air Pollution	Related Legislations
The Environment (Protection) Act, 1986 The Environment (Protection) Rules, 1986 The Manufacture, Storage and Import of Hazardous Chemicals Rules, 1989 The Environment (Protection) Second Amendment Rules, 1992 The Public Liability Insurance Act, 1991 Hazardous Wastes (Management and Handling) Rules, 1989 Rules for the Manufacture, Use, Import, Export and Storage of Hazardous, Micro-Organisms/ Genetically Engineered Organisms or Cells, 1989 *Criminal Law* Criminal Procedure Code Indian Penal Code *Constitutional Law* Related Constitutional provisions	The Water (Prevention and Control of Pollution) Act, 1974 The Water (Prevention and Control of Pollution) Cess Act, 1977	The Air (Prevention and Control of Pollution) Act, 1981	*Water Pollution* The River Boards Act, 1956 The Merchant Shipping (Amendment) Act, 1970 *Air Pollution* The Indian Boilers Act, 1923 The Mines and Minerals (Regulation and Development) Act, 1947 The Factories Act, 1948 (Amended in 1987) The Industrial (Development and Regulation) Act, 1991 Motor Vehicle Act, 1988 Central Motor Vehicle Rules, 1989 (with latest amendment) *Radiation* The Atomic Energy Act, 1962 *Radiation* Protection Rules, 1971 *Others* The Poison Act, 1919 The Insecticides Act, 1968 The Indian Fisheries Act, 1897

contd.

Table I. contd.

General	Water Pollution	Air Pollution	Related Legislations
			The Indian Forest Act, 1927 The Forest (Conservation) Act, 1980 The Prevention of Food Adulteration Act, 1954 The Ancient Monument Archaeological Sites and Remains Act, 1958 The Wild Life Protection Act, 1972 The Urban Land (Ceiling Regulation) Act, 1976 Costal Regulation Zone (CRZ) & Regulation Activities Notification, 1991

Sources: 1. *The Hindu* 'Survey of the Environment' (1992).
2. *The Hindu* 'Survey of the Environment' (1995).
3. A publication of Legal Services Clinic, National Law School of India, Bangalore.
4. *Journal of Social Work*, Vol. LI, No. 1 (January, 1990).
5. Training Course on Costal Zone Management as a sustainable process 17th Oct–16th Dec. 1994, Course Vol. I Reference Material, Indian Institute of Technology, Madras.

in effective implementation of the Acts which is not recognised in any of the laws.

(d) Function of the Authorities

(i) Plan and execute nation wide programmes; carry out and sponsor investigations and research, collection and dissemination of information, preparation of manuals, codes or guides regarding prevention, control and abatement of environmental pollution.

(ii) Lay down standards for quality of environment.

Table II : A Selective List of Environment Related State Enactments

General	Water Pollution	Smoke Control	Pest Control	Land Utilisation and Land Improvement
.....	Orissa River Pollution Prevention Act, 1953	The Bengal Smoke Nuisance Act, 1905	The Mysore Destructive Insects and Pests, Act, 1977	The Andhra Pradesh Improvement Scheme Act, 1949
	Maharashtra Prevention of Water Pollution Act, 1969	The Bombay Smoke Nuisance Act, 1912	The Andhra Pradesh Agricultural Pests and Diseases Act, 1919	The Acquisition of Land and Flood Control and Prevention of Erosion Act, 1955
		The Gujarat Smoke Nuisance Act, 1963	The Assam Agricultral Pests and Diseases Act, 1954	The Delhi Restriction of Uses of Land Act, 1964
			The U.P. Agricultural Pests and Diseases Act, 1958	The Bihar West Lands (Reclamation - Cultivation and Improvement) Act, 1974

Sources: A Publication of Legal Services Clinic, National Law School of India, University, Bangalore and the Indian Journal of Social Work, Vol. LI, No. 1 (January 1990).

(iii) Lay down standards for emission of discharge of environmental pollution.

(iv) Lay down procedures and safeguards for prevention of accidents which may cause environmental pollution and remedial measures for such accidents.

(v) Lay down procedures and safeguards for handling of hazardous substances.

(vi) Demarcate areas in which industries can be set up.

(vii) Examine manufacturing processes, materials and substances that are likely to cause environmental pollution.

(e) Power of the Authorities

(i) Power to give direction which includes the power to direct, prohibit or regulate any industry; stop or regulate supply of electricity or water or any other service.

(ii) Power to enter and inspect any place to perform the functions under the Act.

The authorities under the various Acts have duties and responsibilities without commensurate power to carry out the same. Under the Air and Water Acts, the powers of the Boards are largely advisory in nature. The only measure of control that the authorities can exercise is in granting consent certificates under the Water and Air Acts. However, these provisions are very weak as in that consent is deemed to be given on the expiry of four months in the Water Act and merely on application in the Air Act. Apart from this, there is also overlapping of the powers of the various authorites. While the powers under the Water and Air Acts are exercised by the same Boards, there might be other local authorities such as the municipalities which also have the power to issue industrial licenses. Thus, even if the Water and Air Pollution Boards refused to give consent certificates the same can be obtained from the municipalities. In many States, Boards are yet to be set up as it is not mandatory to set up these Boards. Most of the Boards that have been set up lack sufficient infrastructure to ensure implementation of the Acts.

(f) Remedial Measures

(i) In case of emergencies due to accidents of unforseen events, causing environmental pollution, the Board has the power to take appropriate remedial action.

(ii) In all other instances the Board has to make an application to a court not lower than of a First Class Magistrate.

The scope of remedial measures that can be undertaken by the authorities under the Act is very limited. The Boards have power to undertake remedial action only in the event of accidents or unforeseen occurrences. In the Water Act, apart from these emergency measures, the only power of the Boards is to make an application before the criminal courts. Such a procedure defeats the very purpose of the Act as these Acts have been enacted specifically to overcome the procedural delays and technicalities of the regular criminal courts. Moreover, by restricting action to emergency situations, it hardly provides for any method of effectively implementing the preventive and contr ol measures of the Acts.

In the Environmental Protection Act (EPA), though there is a general mandate not to discharge or remit any environmental pollution in excess of the standards prescribed by the Act, the only remedy that is provided for is by way of penalties and imprisonment which are hardly deterrent in nature. Another major shortcoming is that in all these Acts, the Boards alone can prosecute for violations of the provisions of the Acts which is seldom pursued. In fact there are hardly any instances of prosecutions under these Acts.

Both the Air and Environment Acts provide for the individual to file cases against violations. However, the individuals are required to give 60 days notice to the Government. This requirement makes meaningless the provision of immediate remedial action.

Another provision of the EPA which robs the initiative from effective participation of individuals to safeguard environmental protection is that, which says that, during the 60-days period if the Government itself files a complaint against the industry or communicates to the individual its decision not to file a complaint, the individual cannot proceed with his complaint.

The Acts also bar the jurisdiction of civil courts in all matters of environmental pollution. This bar coupled with the ineffective implementation of the Acts leads to a situation where the public is left with no remedy against environmental pollution. Thus, most industries today get away with impunity, safe with the knowledge that they cannot be prosecuted by individuals in the civil or criminal courts. And the Boards on their part rarely initiate action.

(g) Penalties

(i) Imprisonment which may extent to five months or fine upto Rs. 1 lakh or both.

(ii) In case of continuing offences, Rs. 5,000 per day.

The penalties under the Acts are quite stringent which is welcomed. However, what has to be borne in mind is that in most cases of large companies, these fines, large as they may seem, are meaningless when compared to the cost of compliance of environment standards which is often much more. In this respect the experience of the United Clean Air Act with regard to non-compliance penalties would be of use to us. Under this Act, penalties are measured by the companies in not installing pollution control equipments. So an amount equivalent to the profits gained by non-compliance is imposed. As a result, non-compliance becomes at least as expensive as compliance. This approach has successfully worked in the United States.

The provisions as to imprisonment are totally meaningless. For, while the Directors are made responsible for offences under the Act, they escape punishment if they prove that they are either unaware of the offence or that they exercised due deligence to prevent the commission of such offence. Most large industrial establishments which are mainly responsible for violations are run by huge corporate bodies and it is an impossible task to pin point which individual was responsible for lapses.

An important aspect about these laws that needs to be highlighted is that it nowhere recognises the right to information of citizens. Citizens have neither an access to information with regard to polluting industries nor with regard to action taken by the Government against such offences. Thus, even if individuals are given the right to prosecute offenders under these Acts, these rights cannot be effectively exercised without access to information.

In conclusion, it must be stated while the EPA has been worded in very wide terms to include inter relationships between water, air, land, human beings, other living creatures, plants and micro-organisms, the Act in effect deals only with industrial pollution and hazardous substances. There is no mention of immediate and grave issues such as deforestation, ecological imbalances caused by massive development projects and the destructive potential of large industrial setups including nuclear establishment, thermal plants and mines projects.

In the ultimate analysis, there is a comprehensive policy recognising the complex and mutually interdependent nature of relationships between human beings, nature and environment, any legislation for the protection of environment will remain only an exercise in futulity.

Note: The criticism given at the end of each sub-heading i.e., authorities, function of the authorities, power of the authorities, remedial measures and penalties relate to all the three Acts i.e., The Environment (Protection) Act, 1986, The Water (Prevention and Control of Pollution) Act, 1974 and the Air (Prevention and Control of Pollution) Act, 1981. Hence, the criticism under the Water and Air Acts will not be repeated.

Manufacture, Storage & Import of Hazardous Chemicals (MSI) Rules, 1989 (Amended in 1994)

Bhopal and other similar catastrophic accidents gave rise to a new classification of industries, i.e. those having the potential for major accidents—a major emission, fire or explosion with potential for off-site consequences on human life and the environment. Based on the so-called European Community " Seveso Directive" and legislation enacted by many countries, the MSI Rules enacted in 1989 under the Environment (Protection) Act, 1986 and amended in 1994 represented a comprehensive attempt to regulate major accident hazard (MAH) installations, comprising factories, isolated storages and cross-country pipelines.[12A]

The Rules define hazardous chemicals based on their inherent characterisations of toxicity, flammability and explosivity and also name 432 chemicals in Schedule I. The Rules use the quantity of hazardous chemicals in use in an installation to prescribe three levels of control—low, medium and high.[12B]

Low level controls, which apply to all units using any hazardous chemicals, are required to demonstrate that MAH have been identified and adequate steps taken for prevention, to report major accidents, provide information and training to workers, prepare MSDS for hazardous chemicals and ensure proper labelling of containers. Major accident reporting under these set of rules requires immediate furnishing of a detailed description of location, circumstances, impact within and off-site, short-term alleviatory measures and a subsequent submission of the report on causes, measures for long-term mitigation and prevention of recurrence.[12C]

The more stringent additional controls cover chemicals listed in Schedule II comprising 189 extremely toxic, highly reactive and explosive substances and a fifth category of flammable gases and liquids. The schedule also specifies two levels of threshold quantities of these chemicals, above which the medium and high level controls apply. These controls are also applicable to the isolated storage tanks away from a factory for 27 chemicals in quantities as listed in Schedule III.[12D]

The medium level controls apply at quantities in use above the first threshold quantity. All such sites are required to be notified through the furnishing of information to the authority concerned covering names and quantities of chemicals in use, description of process and storage, organisational structure for ensuring safety and health, MAH identification and control measures and site plans showing chemical inventories and area likely to be affected by a major accident as well as population distribution within.[12E]

High level controls apply to all sites using chemicals above the second threshold quantity and require such sites to prepare and submit a "Safety Report". This is akin to the British "Safety Case" and ensures a comprehensive compilation of all relevant data based on risk assessment and identification of control measures to assist the industry in effective safety management of the MAH site and also enables quick review by the enforcement agencies of the effectiveness of these measures. In addition to the details to be included in the site notification, the safety report covers description process, design's basis and built-in safety features, chemical data, including transformation in the event of abnormal conditions, preliminary hazard analysis including trigger events for major accidents, hazard assessment including known accident history, consequence analysis covering chemical dispersion, potentially affected area and property damage, safety system including maintenance and inspection schedules and training and response and mitigation-related information.[12F]

Mandatory Safety Audit

Vide a 1994 amendment, sites subject to high level controls now have to mandatorily conduct an independent safety audit once a year with the help of an external consultant. The report, along with the management's comments, are required to be furnished to the authority concerned.[12G]

Safety audit is a technique which facilitates independent review of factory's safety programme commissioned by the top management. Earlier being adopted voluntarily, the mandatory requirement will increase the use of this technique in industry. At the same time, development of competency for safety audit in institutions and among individuals is a priority area for action.[12H]

All medium and high level control factories are required to prepare an on-site emergency plan, identify personnel authorised to implement the plan in emergency and train all site personnel in its use. The 1994 amendments also incorporate in Schedule 11 the details to be included in the plan and specify that a mock drill of the plan should be held every six months.

For off-site emergency plan, the Rules designate the District Collector as the District Emergency Authority and empower him along with the concerned MAH sites to formulate the plans. The format of the off-site plan is spelt out in the newly incorporated Schedule 12 and the amendments also require the rehearsal of the off-site plan once a year.[12I]

Periodic mock drills/rehearsals as prescribed will increase the practicality of the plans and ensure maintenance of a state of preparedness. The Rules also stipulate that persons liable to be affected by a major accident are to be informed either by the site management or through the District Emergency Authority about the nature of the hazard and the safety measures do's and don'ts in the event of a major accident in a plant in their neighbourhood.[12J]

The Environment (Protection) Second Amendment Rules, 1992

Under a 1992 amendment to the Environment Protection Rules, Rule 14 requires all industries to obtain consent under the Air and Water Pollution Control Acts to furnish an Annual Environment Statement covering quantities of pollutants discharged, hazardous and solid wastes generated, their characteristics and pollution abatement measures to the State Pollution Control Boards.[12K]

The Water (Prevention and Control of Pollution) Act, 1974

(a) Definition

(i) Contamination of water or alteration of the physical, chemical or biological properties of water.

(ii) Discharge of any sewage or trade effluent or any other liquid, gaseous or solid substance into water.

(iii) This discharge may be direct or indirect and likely to cause nuisance or render such water harmful or injurious to public health or safety or to domestic, commercial, industrial, agriculture or other uses or to the life and health of animals or plants or aquatic organisms.

(b) Objectives

(i) Prevention and control of water pollution maintaining or restoring the wholesomeness of water.

(ii) Creating Board for the above purposes.

(c) Authorities

(i) Central Board:

Appointments are made by the Central Government. The Board consists of:

Table III : Some of the Major Chemical Disasters in India starting from Bhopal

Date of occurrence	Place where occurrence took place	No. of people killed	No. of people affected	Nature of accident
December 2, (midnight) 1994	Union Carbide Bhopal (MP)	Several thousands	Several lakhs	MIC & Toxic gas leak
December, 1985	Shri Ram Food and Fertilisers, Delhi	02	500	Delum gas leak
July, 1987	Bhorari Industrial Area, Pune (Maharashtra)	—	420	Sulphur trioxide leak
June, 1987	Kaluparaghata, Bhubeneswar(Orissa)	04	NA	Amonia Gas leak
November, 1987	Berhampur, Ahmedabad (Gujarat)	—	5000	Oleum gas leak
May, 1988	Dessa Town, Ahmedabad (Gujarat)	19	53	Acid Tanker overturned
October, 1989	Chlorinators India, Ganjam (Orissa)	06	100	Chlorine gas leak
November, 1990	India Petro Chemicals Ltd., Nagothane (Maharashtra)	35	50	Explosion in gas eraker plant
. . . . 1991	Gwalior Rayon and Silk Mills, Gwalior (Madhya Pradesh)	09	100	Explosion in filling unit
November, 1991	Dahanu (Maharashtra)	100	19	Chemical explosion from overturned tanker
April, 1992	Naya Bazar, Delhi	12	—	Chemical explosion in ware house
September, 1992	National Fertilizer Plant, Panipat (Haryana)	11	11	Amonia gas leak
March, 1993	Century Rayon, Sahad (Maharashtra)	11	123	Sulphuric acid gas leak
October, 1994	Jhansi, Uttar Pradesh	30	25	Explosion in a factory

Source: *The Hindu*, Survey of the Environment, 1995, p. 171.

1. A full-time Chairman having specialised knowledge or experience in matters of environmental protection to be nominated by the Central Government.

2. Maximum of five Central Government Officials.
3. Maximum of five State board members.
4. Maximum of three non-officials representing interest of agriculture, trade, fishery and industry.
5. Two representatives of Central Government owned companies or corporation.
6. A full-time member-secretary qualified in 'public health engineering' and having practical experience of environmental protection methods.

(ii) State Boards:

All appointments are made by the State Government concerned.

1. Either a wholetime or part-time Chairman having special knowledge, practical experience or administrative experience or related institution.
2. Maximum of five State Government officials.
3. Maximum of five representatives from among members of local authorities.
4. Maximum of three non-officials representing agriculture, fishery or trade industry.
5. Two representatives of State Government companies or corporations.
6. A full-time Member-Secretary.

Note: Both Central and State Boards are registered corporate bodies who have a legal character, can hold properties and can sue and be sued. The Board members hold office for three years, barring the member-secretary. Board members can be re-nominated only for two extra terms.

(d) Function of the Authorities

(i) To advise, provide technical assistance and guidance, carry out and sponsor investigations and research, plan and organise the training of persons and to organise through mass media comprehensive programme regarding the prevention and control of water pollution.

(ii) To lay down standards for water in streams or wells.

(iii) To establish or recognise laboratories to perform functions including sample analysis.

(e) Powers of Authorities

(i) The power to obtain information from individuals regarding removal or discharge of water as also regarding the construction, installation or operation of any disposal system in establishments where industry or trade is carried on.

(ii) To take samples of water from any stream or well or of any sewage or trade affluent.

(iii) Power to enter and inspect any plant, record, register, document and conduct search of a place if the authority has reason to believe that an offence under the Act has been committed. In residential areas, entry can be only at reasonable hours.

(iv) Power to grant, and inspect for consent with regard to discharge of sewage or industrial effluents; and to impose conditions with regard to discharge.

On application, if there is no response from the authorities, 'unconditional consent' is deemed to have been given on the expiry of four months.

(f) Remedial Measures

(i) In times of emergency when an accident of unforseen event occurs causing pollution, the Board has power to take appropriate remedial action restraining or prohibiting a person from discharging pollution matters. During any such remedial action, reasons have to be recorded in writing.

(g) Penalties

(i) Imprisonment for a period extending to three months or fine upto Rs. 5,000 or both.

(ii) In case of continuing violations, an additional fine extending to Rs. 1000 per day of violation.

The Water (Prevention and Control of Pollution) Cess, Act, 1977

(a) Introduction

This Act has been enacted for the levy and collection of a cess on water consumed by persons carrying on certain industries and by local authorities, with a view to augment the resources of the Centre Board and the State Boards for the prevention and control of water pollution constituted under the Water (Prevention and Control of Pollution) Act, 1974. It extends to all States to which Water Pollution Act, 1974 applied and also to Union territories.

(b) Levy of Cess

A cess is to be levied and collected for purposes of the main Act and for utilisation there under from every person carrying on any specified industry and from every local authority.[13] The specified industry is listed in the 1st Schedule of the Water Cess Act. The cess is calculated on the basis of the water consumed for the purposes specified in the 2nd Schedule, column 1. The maximum rate of cess is laid down in the 2nd Schedule, column 2 and within this maximum, the Central Government can, by notification in the official gazette, specify the rate from time to time.

(c) Measurement of Water

According to Section 4 of the main Act, meters are to be affixed for measuring and recording the quantity of water consumed.

(d) Administrative Matters

The administrative matters are laid down in the Sections 5 to 10 and Section 13 of the Act.

(e) Penalties

(i) For non-payment: Where the cess as levied under the Act is in arrears, the prescribed authority may, after the prescribed inquiry, impose a penalty not exceeding the amount of cess in arrears as per the provision of Section 11 of the Act. But the penalty is not to be imposed if, after hearing, the said authority is satisfied that the default was for any good and sufficient reason. The right to appeal to the prescribed authority has been provided in Section 13 of the Act.

(ii) For submission of false return: There are punishments for submission of false return (Section 14(1) of the Act) and wilful evasion of cess Section 14(2) of the Act. But it is astonishing that there are no punishment for failure to submit the return.

Under Section 14(3), cognigance of an offence under Section 14 cannot be taken without a complaint made by or under the authority of the Central Government.

(f) Offences by Companies

The provision regarding offences by companies is dealt within Section 15 of the Act, but there is no specific provision with regard to local authorities, which is essential.

(g) Schedules and Rules

Section 16 of the Act empowers the Central Government by notification to add industries in the First Schedule. The notification must be laid before Parliament. Section 17 of the same Act confers on the Central Government power to make rules for carrying out the purpose of the Act. Surprisingly the requirement to notify the rules has been left out, which is essential.

The Air (Prevention and Control of Pollution) Act, 1981

(a) Definition

(i) Presence in the atmosphere of any solid, liquid or gaseous substance in such concentration so as to be injurious to human beings or other living creatures or plants or property or environment.

(b) Objectives

(i) Prevention/control and abatement of air pollution.

(ii) Creating Boards for the above purposes.

(c) Authorities

(i) Central Boards: The Central Board for the Prevention and Control of Water Pollution also is the Board appointed under this Act on the same terms and possessing the same powers.

(ii) Both Central and State Air Boards are corporate bodies similar to Water Boards.

Note: The criticism on each of the items mentioned under Water and Air Acts has been mentioned under the EPA. Hence, those are not repeated here.

The Factories Act, 1948 (Amended in 1987)

The Factories Act, 1948 underwent a radical restructuring of its safety and health provisions in 1987, placing increased responsibility on top managements as well as manufacturers and suppliers, a new Chapter regulating hazardous processes, and stipulating workers, involvement in safety management and disclosure of information on hazards.[12L]

Top Management Responsibility

Top management responsibility was provided by redefining the "Occupier"—to be one of the firm's partners: company's director or chief executive office of a State-owned factory. Further, Section 7A places a general duty on the occupier to ensure the health and safety of workers, not merely complying with the detailed technical provisions of the law, but taking a pro-active approach to identify and assess risks and implement effective control measures. This cause is in line with modern safety legislation worldwide, which recognises the limitation of the law in keeping up with technological change and prescribing detailed control measures. It also facilitates prosecution in the event of an accident, even if no specific measure prescribed under law has been contravened. Under this section, managements are required to prepare and publicise their safety policy as well as back it up with the organisation and make arrangements for its implementation.

Similarly, there is a general responsibility on manufacturers and suppliers to design and supply equipment and substances, which are safe and without health risk, as well as information about its safe use. This is an important step in developing concepts of industrial product safety and liability. Further, in case of transactional transfer of technology, parent company safety standards, if more stringent than the relevant Indian standard, are to be followed.[12M]

Safety Measures for Hazardous Processes

A separate Chapter IVA, was introduced to regulate those hazardous Schedule process listed under Schedule I, which used chemicals posing risk to workers' health or having potential for environmental pollution.[12N]

Site Appraisal Committees set up by the State Governments scrutinise all applications for new hazardous plants as well as expansion of existing plants, to assess the risk to the surrounding environment. Establishing on-site emergency plans so as to have effective response and to minimise the consequences of a disaster is another important provision.[12O]

Factory managements have a responsibility to develop Material Safety Data Sheet (MSDSA) for each chemical in use and disclose information regarding the chemicals in use, healthy hazards, safety measures to be adopted as well as action to be taken in the event of an accident, not only to the Factory Inspectorate and local authorities but also to their workers and the public living in the vicinity of their plant. A format of the details of information in each category is given in the Factories Rules enacted in each State.[12P]

Further, each container of a hazardous substance is required to be appropriately labelled.[12Q]

Health Record of Workers

Periodic medical examination of workers exposed to toxic or other harmful substances are required to be carried out and the health records made available to workers on request. Further recognising the long latency period of many occupational diseases, such examinations are required to be continued even after a worker has ceased to work on that job.[12R]

Schedule II which prescribes the permissible levels of 123 chemical substances in the work environment has been an important step in introducing periodic monitoring of the work environment and consequent steps to reduce workplace pollution.[12S]

Joint worker-management safety committees are now mandatory in all hazardous industries as well as in other factories employing over 250 workers. The composition of such committee, election of workers representatives, tenure periodicity of meetings and functions and duties are laid down under the Factories Rules of each State. The scope of such committees is wide ranging and includes opportunity to discuss all matters of safety, health and environment including implementation of management commissioned safety surveys, audits and risk assessments.[12T]

Under Section IIIA, all workers are given the right to obtain information on their safety and health, to receive training and approach the Factory Inspector either directly or through his representative for adequate provision of safety and health protection. Further, in hazardous factories, in the event of apprehension of imminent danger to their lives or health, workers have the right to complain to the management, directly or through the Safety Committee and simultaneously to the Factory Inspector.[12U]

Central Motor Vehicles Rules, 1989

The last decade has seen several accidents involving explosions of vehicles transporting flammable substances. The accidents in Mendhwan (1991–96 deaths) and Kawathe 1987–34 deaths) involving uneducated villagers are tragic reminders of the risks which such transportation poses. Maharashtra was the first State to regulate such a situation by incorporating additional permit conditions in the Motor Vehicle Rules, which subsequently became the basis for national-level requirements.

The Central Motor Vehicles Rules, 1989, incorporate a series of requirements for vehicle transporting hazardous chemicals and placed responsibility on the consignor/owner for:

- display of diamond-shaped class labels containing Class No. and graphic symbols of the chemicals as per U.N. Classification for transport of dangerous goods;
- display of Emergency Information Panel at three places on each vehicle containing name, U.N. No. Hazchem Code, Class label, telephone number of emergency service to be contacted and brief specialist advice regarding transportation emergency response;
- carrying of Transport Emergency Cards (TREM Cards) specifying nature of hazard and type of response required; and
- placing responsibility on driver to take precaution to prevent accidents, proper parking and appropriate action in event of emergency.

A further amendment to these Rules in 1993 provides for a system of driver training and certification, including the syllabus for a three-day course for such drivers.

The labelling to tankers, provision of TREM Cards and establishing a system of driver training through uneven implementation have focused attention on the problem and set in motion a framework for safe transportation and response, which is to be further developed.

The Public Liability Insurance Act, 1991

The Public Liability Insurance Act, was enacted with a view to make it a regulatory measure of the greatest significance for business and industry. It has two objectives, such as (i) "no fault" liability, for harm caused while handling any hazardous substance, (ii) for such liability, it is made compulsory to take out liability insurance. The first objective makes an important modification in the principle of tort liability as applicable to such accidents.

The rule of *Rylands* and *Fletcher*[13] which had been followed in India by the decisions of a number of High Courts,[14] has been overruled by the Supreme Court in *M.C. Mehta* v. *Union of India*.[15] The apex court has enunciated a new principle of liability saying:

> "We are of the view that an enterprise which is engaged in a *Hazardous* or *inherently dangerous* industry which poses a potential threat to the health and safety of the persons working in the factory and residing in the surrounding areas *owns an absolute and nondelegable duty* to the community to ensure that no harm results to any one on account of hazardous or inherently dangerous nature

of the activity which it has undertaken. The enterprise must be held to be under an obligation to provide that the hazardous or inherently dangerous activity in which it is, must be conducted with the *highest standards of safety* and if any harm results on account of such activity, the enterprise must be absolutely liable to compensate for such harm and it should be no answer to the enterprise to say that it had taken all reasonable care and that the harm occurred without any negligence on its part. Since the persons harmed on account to the hazardous or inherently dangerous activity carried on by the enterprise would not be in a position to isolate the process of operation from the hazardous preparation or substance or any other related element that caused the harm, the enterprise must be held *strictly liable* for causing harm as a part of the social cost of carrying on the hazardous or inherently dangerous activity. If the entrprise permitted to carry on hazardous or inherently dangerous activity for its profit, the law must presume that such permission is conditional on the enterprise absorbing the cost of any accident arising on account of such hazardous or inherently dangerous activity as an appropriate item of its overheads. Such hazardous or inherently dangerous activity indemnified all those who suffer on account of the carrying on of such hazardous or inherently dangerous activity, regardless of whether it is carried on carefully or not. This principle is also sustainable on the ground that the enterprise alone has the resource to discover and guard against hazards or dangers and to provide warnings against potential hazards. We would, therefore, hold that where an enterprise is engaged in a hazardous or inherently dangerous activity and harm results to anyone on account of an accident in the operation of such hazardous an inherently dangerous activity resulting, for example, in the escape of toxic gas, the enterprise is *strictly* and *absolutely* liable to compensate all those who are affected by the accident and such liability is not subjected to any of the exceptions which operate vis-a vis the fortuitous principle of strict liablity under the rule in *Rylands* v. *Fletcher*."

The gist of the Public Liability Insurance Act, 1991 is as follows:

(a) The Public Liability Insurance Act, 1991 consists of 23 Sections and one schedule. Short title and commencements of the Act are dealt within Section 1, while Section 2 contains several definitions. The substantive provisions of the Act are mainly contained in Sections 3 and 4. Section 3 incorporates the principles of liability without fault for death of injury to any person (other than a workman) or damage to any property, resulting from an accident—"accident" having been defined in Section 2 (a) as meaning, *inter alia*, an accident occurring while handling any hazardous substance. It is against this liability that Section 4 of the Act makes it mandatory for the owner (that is to say, the person who owns or has control over handling any hazardous substance), to take out one or more insurance policies whereby such owner is insured against the liability imposed by Section 3(1).

(b) Section 4(2A) and succeeding sub-sections make certain detailed provisions as to the contents of the policies. By Section 4(3), the Central Government is empowered to grant exemption from the duty to take out an insurance policy. But this is conditional on the establishment and maintenance, by the owner, of a fund for meeting the liability imposed by Section 3(1).

(c) Section 5 to 7 of the Public Liability Insurance Act deal with the preliminary formalities and procedure for applications for claims for relief under the Act. Section 5 requires the Collector to verify the occurrence of an accident, if it comes to his notice, and to cause publicity to be given to it for inviting applications for claims for relief. Section 6 deals with the manner of making such applications and also prescribes a time limit of five years for making such applications. The inquiry into the application by the Collector, and the award of relief by him, are matters dealt within Section 7, which also provides that the amount awarded shall be recoverable as arrears of land revenue or of public demands. Section 7A (inserted in 1992), provides for the creation of Environmental Relief Fund.

(d) Section 8 saves any other right to claim compensation in respect of death, injury to person or damage to property under any other law for the time being in force. Certain powers necessary for the working of the Act are dealt with, in Sections 9,10 and 11, relating to calling for information, entry and inspection and search and seizure. A very important provision, contained in Section 12, is to the effect that the Central Government may issue written directions "for the purpose of the Act," to any owner or any other person and regulating the handling of any hazardous substance or a direction stopping or regulating the supply of "electricity, water or any other service." By Section 13, the Central Government or an authorised person is also given power to apply to the court for an order restraining the owner handling any hazardous substances in contravention of the Act.

(e) Sections 14 to 18 deal with offences, penalties and procedural provisions connected therewith. By Section 19, the Central Government is empowered to delegate its powers under the Act, excepting the rule-making power. Section 20 protects action taken in good faith under the Act. Section 21 provides for an advisory committee on matters relating to insurance policies under the Act. Section 22 gives to this Act an overriding effect. Power to make rules is given to the Central Government by Section 23.

(f) The Schedule to the Act gives a tariff of compensation to be awarded as a result of the liability provided for in Section 3(1) of the Act.

Laws and Their Implementation

The main legislations on control of environmental pollution which are presently being administered by the Union as well as State Governments and the Central and State Pollution Control Boards are:

i) The Water (Prevention and Control of Pollution), 1974 (amended in 1978 and 1988).
ii) The Water (Prevention and Control of Pollution) Cess Act, 1977 (amended in 1991).
iii) The Air (Prevention and Control of Pollution) Act, 1981 (amended in 1987).
iv) The Environmental (Protection) Act, 1986.
v) The Public Liability Insurance Act, 1991.

If the Water, Air and Environment Acts are taken together, polluting units can be closed, or their water and electricity supply discontinued. But these clauses are never invoked by the implementing agencies, which are the State Pollution Control Boards. These Boards instead of controlling pollution are causing pollution. Hence, they are called as "Pollution Causing Boards"

The laws were entrusted with ineffective, untrained and sometimes corrupt staff, who did not have any commitment towards controlling pollution. Members appointed to these boards have more to do with politics than preservation of the environment.

The most glaring example of the inefficient functioning of these boards is that a few weeks before the Bhopal gas tragedy, the pollution control equipment of Union Carbide Limited had been granted a clearance by the Madhya Pradesh Pollution Control Board.

Besides the above, several provisions of the Acts are also being misused or misinterpreted, which defeat the very objective of the laws. The Environment Protection Act, 1986, for instance, allows for community action against companies responsible for polluting the environment. A sixty days notice is required to be given to the State Pollution Board before filing a suit against the industrial unit.[16] This Provision is often misused. A notice may never be given if the people do not known the law, and they would, thus, not be able to go to court. But even if a notice is given, the boards simply ignore it.

The evidence required to convict a polluting industry in terms of air and water samples has to be collected by the board authorities.[17] This means that an unwilling board can stall the proceedings by not taking samples at all.

Likewise, the Factories Act[18] stipulates that submitting a detailed disaster management plan is mandatory for hazardous units, which must be produced on demand by any member of the public. Yet, this never happens. Even public sector companies flout this provision and the law remains only on paper. No individual can ever obtain the disaster management plan, which in many cases in not available. For many units, the Official Secrets Act is invoked and the stock reply is given that it is not in the public interest to know these things. Nuclear plants and power projects have traditionally done this kind to stonewalling.

REFERENCES

1. Environment, Development and Law in Developing Countries, address Mr. Justice A.M. Ahmadi, Judge, Supreme Court of India & Hony. President of International Jurist Organisation (Asia), who presided over the inaugural session, Legal Aid Newsletter vol. xii (Part 3 & 4), October 92–Mar. 93, p. 15.
2. Jariwala C.M., *Direction of Environmental Justice in India: Critical Appraisal of 1987 Case Laws*, JILI vol. 35 (1 & 2), p. 92.
3. *Supra* note 1 at page 2.
4. *Supra* note 2.
5. Sections 188, 263–294A of the Indian Penal Code.
6. Sections 133–143 and 357 of the Criminal Procedure Code.
7. Sections 9 and 91 of the Code of Civil Procedure.
8. See 'absolute liability', 'strict liability' and 'tort liability'.
9. *Suresh* v. *Nagasaila D. and Geetha D.*, Environmental Protection Laws, *The Hindu Survey of Environment*, 1992, p. 165.
10. *Ibid.*
11. *Ibid.*
12. This Act in view of its importance, has been dealt with in a separate chapter in detail.

12A. The Hindu, Survey of the Environment, 1995, pp. 168–69.
12B. *Ibid.*
12C. *Ibid.*
12D. *Ibid.*
12E. *Ibid.*
12F. *Ibid.*
12G. *Ibid.*
12H. *Ibid.*
12I. *Ibid.*
12J. *Ibid.*
12K. *Ibid.*
12L. *Ibid.*
12M. *Ibid.*
12N. *Ibid.*
12O. *Ibid.*
12P. *Ibid.*
12Q. *Ibid.*
12R. *Ibid.*
12S. *Ibid.*
12T. *Ibid.*
12U. *Ibid.*
13. (1868) L.R.I. Ex. 265, 279, 280.
14. *Ramanuja Chariar* v. *Krishnaswami Mundali*, (1907) ILR 31, Mad. 169; *Dhanusa* v. *Sitabai*, ILR (1948) Nag. 698; *M. Madappa* v. *K. Karappa*, AIR, 1964 Nay 80; *Mukesh Textile Mills Pvt. Ltd.* v. *Subramanya Sastry,* AIR, 1987, Karn. 887.
15. AIR, 1987 SC 1086.
16. Section 19(b) of the Environment Protection Act, 1986.
17. Section 12(2) (b) *ibid.*
18. Section 7A of the Factories Act, 1948 (amended in 1987).

CHAPTER IV

FOREST AND WILDLIFE PROTECTION

Deforestation and Environmental Degradation

The relentless destruction of the forests is destroying many lives in our country, particularly of those people who live in remote villages and tribal belts. These days deforestation has almost become synonymous with environmental deterioration. It is not an astonishing thing so far as the India's forests are concerned. The National Forest Policy of 1952, as well as the National Commission on Agriculture (NCA) 1976, have stipulated an optimum requirement of 33 per cent forest area of the total land mass. However, the 1980–82 satellite picture confirmed a tree cover of only 14.1 per cent. Today according to the Department of Environment, only 10.63 or 35 million of the country's 329 million hectare are under tree cover (anon. 185a). Satellite photographs had shown a tree cover of 16.8 per cent in 1972–75, indicating a subsequent loss of 34 per cent in the decade 1974–84. The National Remote Sensing Agency confirmed in mid 1984, that the annual loss of tree cover is a staggering 1.3 million ha (CSE 1985:80). It may be noted that India accepts land with 30 per cent tree cover as forest area while the international criterion is 40 per cent. If one were to accept the international criterion, the actual area under tree cover in India would be reduced considerably.[1]

The statistical data mentioned above may be considered as *ad hoc.* The reason is that the satellite picture taken from time to time by different data sources varies. The table given on next page, compiled and published by the Statistical Branch of the Office of the Principal Chief Conservator of Forests, Orissa, Bhubaneswar (1990) gives an idea of the variation marked from time to time.

Table 1 : Forest Area: Density Classes (Vegetation Cover)

Period	Closed (40% and above)	Open (10% to below 40%)	Mangrove	Total	Data Source	Reference
1972–75	37320	10829	234	48383	KSS	NRSA 1983
1975–77	34350	20850	—	55890	KSS	FAO 1981
1980–82	28812	10386	227	39425	KSS	NRSA 1983
Oct–Dec 1981	28573	24391	199	53163	KSS	FSI 1987
Nov–Dec 1987	27561	19384	192	47137	TK	FSI 1989
Nov–Dec 1989	27349	19661	195	47205	TK	FSI 1991

Historical Development

A historical survey of the forest will give us some insight into the mistakes committed in the past regarding forests in India. Before the advent of the British rule in India, there was only customary regulation of people's right over forest land and forest produce. This did not pose any problem due to the existence of vast tracts of forests and small population. Custom prohibited cutting of certain trees like *banyan* and *pipal*. Certain forests called Devaranya (God's groves) were regarded as sacred and were protected. People were supposed to use only the fallen leaves and fruit and not to cut any tree therein. This helped the conservation of natural forests with all their gamut of living organism.[2]

In other parts of India, sacredness attached to the preservation of the most valuable trees took different forms. In the Tehri-Garwal region, for example, many restrictions were placed on the collection of firewood from the community forests. In the dry Aravalli hills, in forests known as Orany, the use of axe was completely forbidden and harvest was restricted to what could be broken by hand. The Bishnoi community in Rajasthan placed similar restrictions to protect their most valuable trees *Prosopis cinerarea* (Gadgil 1982). Obviously, industrial demand was low and conservation was relatively easy since commercialisation was limited to sandal wood, ivory and similar luxury items.[3]

The situation was changed with colonialism. In colonial times, forests were viewed mainly as a commercial resource. Most scholars accept that the process of deforestation commenced during the British rule. The primary aim of the colonisers was to utilise the resources of the colony to meet the industrial requirements in their home country and the administrative expenditure in the colony. Destruction of natural resources no doubt formed a part of their colonial policies.[4]

With the pressure mounting on the British Government to meet the revenue requirements of the colony, especially the expenditure on the army, which had increased from 41.9 per cent of India's budget in 1900 to 51.9 per cent in 1904–05, the colonial government was forced to fall back on the forests, since it could not resort to further taxation on land for the fear of repraisal from the land lords. The forest could be easily exploited because no such repraisal were to be expected from the tribals who lacked any bargaining power.[5] The British government reserved to itself, rights over large tracts of forest till then owned by local communities. Many tribals and other forest dwellers opposed this "violent confiscation of the long cherished rights of the people."[6] In Bombay, Senapati Bapat led a revolt against the submersion of vast forest tract in the Bombay state by a dam built by the Tatas. However, those revolts were quickly crushed and even ended in massacres, as in the case of Tiludi in Tehri state in 1930.[7]

In 1894 the government reviewed its Forest Policy and stated in clear terms that:[8]

(i) The sole object with which state forests are administered is public benefit. In general, the constitution and preservation of the forest involve the regulation of rights and the restriction of the privileges of the user in the forest by the neighbouring population;

(ii) Forest situated on hill slopes should be maintained as protected forests to preserve the climate and physical conditions of the country and to protect the cultivated plains that lie below them from the devastating action of hill torrents;

(iii) Forests which are the reservoirs of valuable timbers should be managed on commercial lines as a source of revenue to the state;

(iv) Wherever the effective demand for cultivable land exists and can only be supplied by forest area, the land should ordinarily be relinquished without hesitation, subject to the following conditions:

(a) Honeycombing of a valuable forest by patches of cultivation would not be allowed;

(b) Cultivation must be permanent and must not be allowed to an extent as to encroach upon the minimum area of forest that is needed to meet the reasonable forest requirements, present and prospective; and

(c) Forests that yield only inferior timber, fuelwood or fodder or are used for grazing should be managed mainly in the interest of the local population, care being taken to see that the use is not exercised so as to annihilate its subject and the people are protected against their own improvidence.

Thus, the policy emphasised the commercial use of the forest has also its ecological value. It paved the way for the regulation of rights and privileges of forest dwellers over forest land and produce. What is important to bear in mind is that the only rationality behind this policy was commercial needs and revenue collection.

India won independence in 1947, after a prolonged struggle, the Indian people overthrew the colonial yoke. But the reins of power passed out of hands of the mercenary mercantile interests of Britishers into the hands of their Indian counterparts. The similar interests of the new Indian ruling class ensures, however, that the forest policy continued in essence as laid down by the colonial overlords. The Government of India adopted the National Forest Policy wherein it reiterated vehemently the grave need of protection of forests and categorised forests of India into four categories, namely, Protected Forests, National Forests, Village Forests, and Treelands. The State Governments were left unfettered in forest administration, provided that it was in consonance with the Centre's forest policy for preservation and development of the nation's forest resources.

National Forest Policy, 1952

The National Forest Policy, 1952 is an important turning point in the evolution of forest management in India. By 1952, wood based industries such as pulp, paper and plywood were well established, and their demand for raw material became an important consideration in the management of forests. Obviously, increasing demand from these sectors results in conflicts. The 1952 Forests Policy clearly recognises this aspect and points out that local interest and priorities should be subservient to the broader national interests. The Government of India while upholding said;

> "Village communities in the neighbourhood of a forest will naturally make a greater use of its production for the satisfaction of their domestic and agricultural needs. Such use, however, should in no events be permitted at the cost of national interest.[9]

In a way, this was an extension of the colonial British policy and laid down that the claims of the communities living in and near forests should not override national interest.

In actual practice, the concept of national interest was interpreted in a very narrow sense. The destruction of forests for the construction of roads, buildings, irrigation and hydro-electricity project, ammunition factories and other projects was justified in the name of national interest. Whereas cultivation of lands shown as forest lands, but without any actual tree cover, was treated as encroachment. *Adivasis* living near forests were discouraged from using forests whenever possible. The Government tried to obtain more and more revenue from the forests. India's technically skilled professional forest service personnel treated *adivasis* as the enemies of the forests.

Legislative Measures

The first legislation to give effect to rules for the management and preservation of government forests was passed in 1865.[10] The Act empowered the government to declare by notification any land covered with trees, brush-wood or jungle as government forest. Section 2 of the Act provided that such notification should not abridge or affect any existing rights of individuals or communities. The government was empowered to make rules relating to the preservation of trees etc. The local governments (which are now called as State governments) were authorised to make rules relating to preservation of trees etc. and were empowered to prescribe punishments for the breach of the provisions of the Act. Rules were laid down for confiscation of implements used in the offences and for arrest of the offenders. The major objective of the provisions of the Act was to establish governmental control over forest. The above Act was repealed by the Indian Forest Act, 1878. This was more comprehensive than the earlier Act. According to the 1878 Act, forests were divided into three categories such as (i) reserve forests, (ii) protected forests and (iii) village forests.

Persons were to be notified to prefer their claims over land and forest produce in the proposed reserved forests. The Forest Settlement Officer was empowered to acquire land over which rights were claimed by persons. The Forests Settlement Officer was to record such rights and there were special provisions to ensure the exercise of such rights. These provisions included setting out some other forest tract to ensure the right of pasture or the right to forests produce, altering the limit of the proposed forest so as to exclude forest land of sufficient extend, for the purpose of claimants and proper recording in order to ensure 'claimants' rights in certain portions of the proposed reserved forest.[11] Certain Acts like trespass or pasturing of cattle were prohibited in the reserved forests. The local government were given right to notify any forest or land as protected forest after ascertaining the nature and the extent of the right of government and of private persons in and over the forests land or wasteland comprised therein. They were also empowered to make rules to regulate and prohibit certain Acts in protected forests.

Certain provisions were made to regulate or prohibit certain Acts damaging trees over forests and lands that were not the property of the government. Thus the 1878 Act continued and extended the government policy of establishing control over forests. It also made general provision for the imposition of duty on timber.

The Indian Forest Act of 1878 was modified in parts by different Acts of the local governments. It was later on replaced by a very comprehensive Act called the 'Indian Forest Act, 1927.' The new Act brought together all the major provisions of the earlier ones including those relating to the duty on timber.

The Government of India Act of 1935, passed by the British Parliament, created provincial legislatures. The subject of forests was included in the provincial legislative list under the Act. Thereafter several provinces made their own laws to regulate forests. Most of these laws were within the framework laid down in the 1927 Act.[12]

Forest was a subject in the State List in the 7th schedule of the Constitution of India, which came into force on 26th January, 1950. It continued as such till 1976. It was transposed from the State List to the Concurrent List by the 42nd Amendment in 1976.[13] This resulted in the diminition of the State's power. The Union government used its power drastically to curtail State's rights over forests. Subsequently, the Forest (Conservation) Ordinance was promulgated in 1980[14] to make certain reforms over the proceeding Act of 1927 which had imposed restrictions on the reservation of forests or use of forest land for non-forest purpose by the State. The ordinance was later on converted into an Act known as the Forest (Conservation) Act, 1980.[15] Section 2 of the Act provides:

> "No State Government or other authority shall make (except with the prior approval of the Central Government) directions that: (1) any reserved forests (within the meaning of expression 'reserved forests' in any law for the time being in force in that state) or any portion thereof shall cease to be reserved; (ii) that any forest, land or any portion thereof may be used for any non-forest purpose."[16]

Despite such laws, it has been experienced that in number of states (Karnataka, U.P., Bihar and West Bangal) forests are being denuded indiscriminately. The main reasons of this deforestation appear to be as given below:[17]

(i) Inactiveness on the part of officers, under the law, who are the custodians and guardians of forests seems to be the main cause. The strong groups or private contractors fell trees either at the connivance of authorities or by gratifying them or by exercise of political pressure. It is true that the bureaucrats, officials of forest department, big contractors and industrialists are parties to this collusion, devastating the forests. Dual policy of government is also responsible for deforestation because the lands, out of which the tribes and villagers were given firewood at cheap rates, are now being given to industrialists to establish industries, in violation of law. Big contractors are given relief and relaxation in tree felling to get timber for furniture manufacturing. Thus, the villagers and tribals are divested of their rights. Bihar Government is receiving 876.65 lakh of rupees as forest revenue for the past few years, but there is no increase of revenue inspite of increase in rate of tree felling. It is due to rampant corruption amongst forest authorities.[18]

(ii) Equally important is the need of people, which is resulting in deforestation. Immense industries, trucks, car, engines and buses, etc. consume a lot of petroleum, coal and electricity, etc., and in addition to it lion's share is held by wood as fuel, being used in cooking. Despite the massive development of oil and coal resources, non-commercial energy sources like firewood, agricultural wastes and cowdung are crucial for India's energy. In 1975–76, 28 per cent of total energy consumed in India came from 133 million tonnes of firewood. Therefore, the one reason of deforestation is its use as source of energy.

(iii) Deforestation for commercial purposes like manufacture of furniture, body of vehicles, shops or packings of fruits or sports goods, etc. Much greater damage, however, has been done in recent years by the commercial approach of forest department which has led to the cutting down of the rice natural forests for planting of teak and eucalyptus and starting of certain forest-based industries like plywood and paper in the district along with contracting to supply wood at cheap rates to industries located elsewhere like match factories and rayon pulp factory.[19]

(iv) Land consolidation imbibed a sense of insecurity in the minds of farmers with regard to getting their existing fields. Therefore, they removed their trees in fields.

(v) Unawarness as to the importance of forests prevailed for quite a long time which kept the people indifferent regarding forests.

(vi) Large scale urbanization, colonization and industrialization and construction of roads and water canals and drains destroyed a large area of forests. We have heard of controversy over construction of dam in silent valley of Kerala covering 9000 hectares. And this decade old project which has consumed some Rs. three crores has been dropped after a prolonged tussle. With the decision not to build a dam in the valley, silent valley and its unique flora and fauna are safe from human interference. But the questions raised about development *versus* environment continue to be important. Are the considerations of ecology relevant to a developing country? Can we afford to destroy an irreplaceable eco-system which took 50 million years to evolve.[20]

There is no doubt that the development process will lead to deforestation. The need of the hour is to create balance between deforestation and development. The grassroot level movements like Chipko Andolan, Bhoomi Sena, Silent Valley Movement, Jharkhand Movement can do a lot in conservation of environment as they recognise that development and environment go concurrently.

The serious condition of environment due to deforestation and many other things, has time and again evoked various responses from the Government. These reactions have found expression in the enactment of several legislations,[21] in addition to the legislations discussed above, which are directly or indirectly connected with deforestation and environmental degradation. The State of Orissa has also enacted legislations[22] with regard to the above subject.

It is alleged that these attempts are only half-hearted measures which have not been adequately conceptualised and effectively enforced. The Draft Forest Bill, 1980, for instance, elicited such strong reaction from environmentalists and other concerned citizens, that it had to be shelved. To fill up these lacuna the Government enacted the legislations mentioned earlier.

The Constitution of India[23] requires the State to take steps to protect and improve the environment and to safeguard the forest and wild life of the country. Relying upon the same, the Supreme Court in *M.C. Mehta* v. *Union of India*,[24] gave directions to the Central and the

State governments and various local bodies and Boards, under the various statutes, to take appropriate steps for the prevention and control of pollution of water. The Constitution imposes duties upon the State for the improvement of public health.[25] Purity of the air we breathe in and the water we drink is absolutely essential for good health.[26] Equally important is the environment in which we live and work. In view of this, Article 51 A (g) of the Constitution also introduced by the 42nd amendment lays down the following:

> "It shall be the duty of every citizen of India to protect and improve the natural environment including forests, lakes, rivers and wild life, and to have compassion for living creature."

Judicial Response

The legislations enacted to prevent deforestation and degradation of environment are not alone the safety valves against oppression and destruction of forests, the judiciary, specially, the Supreme Court of India has also not lagged behind in coming to the rescue of the people in saving environment.[27]

There are a number of environmental cases, but very few of these cases relate to deforestation and environmental degradation. Before I discuss these cases, I hope that all the environmentalists would be familiar with the name of Mr. M.C. Mehta, who deserves appreciation for the social services he has rendered by filing many important cases[28] in the Supreme Court. He is a senior advocate of the Supreme Court. He has been rightly pointed by the court, "though lone and single" he has fought a valiant battle against a giant enterprise and achieved substantial success. Really, in the present world which has more commercialised rather than socialised approach, it is very difficult to find a social service lawyer who is like an oasis in the desert.[29]

In *Calcutta Youth Front* v. *State of West Bengal*,[30] the Calcutta Municipal Corporation granted licence for a period of 30 years to build and construct a two-storeyed underground air-conditioned basement market on the sub-soil of the Satynarayan Park in the congested locality of Bara Bazar. The environment-conscious public-spirited Calcutta Youth Front took the plea that such construction activities would affect the ecological balance of the area. The single judge of the Calcutta High Court, whose opinion is endorsed by the Division Bench of the same court and also by the Supreme Court, repelled the petioner's above contention. The learned single judge, negativing the contention, opined that the construction work would not destroy the instrinsic character of the park. The only difference would be that the existing park was on ground level and the new one would be on an elevated level. And thus, the single judge opined that it would not cause any ecological imbalance. The learned judge also took notice of the fact that the park was for about a decade, in a deplorable state due to non-maintenance and further that it had not a blade of grass. The supplementary affidavit which was taken into consideration by the court, also stated that the respondent entered into a contract for re-laying of the park as a terrace garden with spacious lawn with fast growing tall and dwarf trees. In view of these facts, the contention of ecological imbalance was rejected. The present construction work instead of adversely affecting the ecology, the learned judge opined, would on the contrary ensure the creation of a green belt.[31]

The above view was also endorsed by the Supreme Court and the court refuted the apprehension expressed by the petitioner's advocate, that the tall trees would disappear from the park. It may be submitted that a terrace garden cannot be considered a suitable place for growing tall trees. They cannot live long in the absence of deep soil. Moreover, their roots will definitely spoil the basement structure, and even though the court was assured of planting such trees, no architecture will allow such a plan on a long term basis. If the big trees are missing from a thickly populated area like Bara Bazar in the instant case, it would lose manifold benefits which such trees provided, like, balance of ecology, absorber of noise pollution, changing the direction of wind and habitat for the birds, etc. A patch of green grass and tall trees cannot be equated with each other while measuring the environmental impact. Thus, in view of the micro-specialist problem, it is submitted that the court should have taken the opinion of an expert rather than go by the assumption of the respondent's counsel.[32]

Thus, in the instant case, the judiciary, right from the single Bench of the Calcutta High Court of the Division Bench of the Supreme Court, tilted the balance in favour of the development process and that too, for a city like Calcutta which is badly polluted.[33]

Another blow to the ecology of Calcutta was in *Sachidananda Pandey* v. *State of West Bengal*.[34] In this case, the Government of West Bengal gave on lease, to Taj Group, four acres of land belonging to the Calcutta Zoological Garden for the construction of a five star hotel. This garden was located in Alipore, the heart of Calcutta. It was this giving away of the land that was challenged by two citizens of Calcutta; one, the Secretary of the Union of Workmen of the Zoological Garden, and the other, a life member of the zoo, claiming themselves to be lovers of wild life and well wishers of the zoo. One of the submission made by the counsel for the appellants was that, the construction of five star hotel was too heavy a cost to pay for the environmental detriment caused by it. But the respondent's counsel submitted that the landscaping was so designed as to encourage tourism, improve and not to disturb the ecology of the place.

The court, dismissing the appeal, took the stand that: [35]

> "If the Government is alive to the various considerations requiring thought and deliberation and has arrived at a conscious decision after taking them into account, it may not be for this court to interfere in the absence of malafides."

A liberal approach in favour of the development process is further reflected when it says: [36]

> "When the question involves the nice balancing of relevant considerations, the court may feel justified in resigning itself to acceptance of the decision of the concerned authority."

It may be pointed out that the Public Undertaking Committee, appointed by the West Bengal Legislative Assembly, the Chief Town Planner and the Forest Department did not approve of the said plan. Even the Managing committee of the zoo was initially of the opinion that such construction would be highly detrimental to the animals of the zoo, migratory birds and its ecological balance. Late Indira Gandhi, the then Prime Minister of India, also at one time directed the Chief Minister of West Bengal "to leave the Calcutta zoo intact." In view of the above materials before the court, it is submitted that it should have handled the matter more seriously. The development of tourism, and few rupees to the exchequer must not be the such important considerations to affect the ecological balance.[37]

There is one more dimension of this judgement wherein discussion of the directive principles and the fundamental duty relating to environment, as usual, finds a place.[38] But the Supreme Court has yet to deal elaborately with these two aspects and further their inter-relationship and also their relationship with the fundamental right to live in a clean environment.

The case of *Damodar Rao* [39] decided by the Andhra Pradesh High Court has taken a different turn though this is in the line of construction cases. The court has gone as far as to interpret environmental pollution as an infringement of Article 21 of the Constitution which enshrines right to life as a fundamental right. In the instant case, an attempt was made by some government departments to build residential houses in an area reserved under the Master Plan for parks. The court held:

> "the enjoyment of life and its attainment by Article 21 of the Constitution embraces the protection and preservation of nature's gift without which life cannot be enjoyed. The slow poisoning caused by environmental pollution and the spoliation should also be regarded as violative of Article 21 . . . ."

Some Suggestions

In view of the above, the following are submitted to avoid deforestation and save the environment from degredation:

1. There is a move by the inter-state council to get more power over the forest. It the powers are transferred to the States, forest officers of the states, it is feared, will not be able to withstand the pressures from their respective Chief Ministers for clearance of what seems a small forest area of five hectares. If 10 to 15 five-hectare plots are cleared, the actual loss of forest land would be 50 to 75 hectares.[40] The Forest Conservation Act of 1980 was amended in 1985 to prevent diversion of forest land for nonforest purposes. This had slowed down the erosion of our forest cover. The purpose of the Act would be lost if the powers with the centre over forests are slowly whittled down or handed over to the States. Instead, the number of Chief Conservators of Forests should be increased and whip given that all cases for forest diversion should be resolved in three months, failing which,.the centre forfiets the rights to clear the proposal.[41] In very hard case, the joint management programme which has been adopted by 14 states can be accepted. The said programme should be carried on under the strict supervision of the çertre. The proposed bill of 1994 to replace the Forest Act of 1927 has also suggested the concentration of power with the central government and its officers. This is welcomed.

2. The Forest Policy of 1988 was issued by the Government of India, revising the earlier Policy of 1952. In order to incorporate some new concepts, the provisions of Indian Forest Act, 1927 have to be amended. The proposed bill of 1994 to replace the Indian Forest Act, 1927 does not incorporate fully the basic principles of the Forest Policy, 1988 where it has been specifically mentioned that the people's interests would take precedence over commercial interests. In this connection, a seminar held very recently, on the occasion of the World Forest Day on March

24, 1995 in India having been organised by the Economic Development Institute (EDI) of the World Bank, has also suggested: [42]

> "Government has failed to stop the destruction of forests, in fact it has become widespread. One way to solve this problem would be to adopt a new approach—rely more on the people, make them look after the forests and enjoy the fruits."

Hence, it is submitted that this seminar should recommend the above view to the Government for its inclusion in the proposed amendment Act.

3. The law by itself is inadequate to bring about the desired change in society without public awareness and participation in the process. Unfortunately, lack of awareness and apathy of the people towards environmental concerns, are on the grave consequences of ignoring environmental priorities, have acted against changing the situtation.[43] A step to retrieve this situation was taken by the Supreme Court in *M.C. Mehta* v. *Union of India*,[44] where the apex court has directed the district collectors to ensure exhibition of two slides on environment and pollution in cinema halls and video parlours as a condition for issueing license for these establishments. Doordarshan and All India Radio have been directed to produce daily programmes with a duration of five to seven minutes with messages on the environment and a regular weekly programme on the subject.[45] In this connection, it is submitted that, the programmes which are being shown daily in different T.Vs., should be slightly more narrative, so that an ordinary person can easily understand.

4. The environmentalists, all over the country, must be grateful to the Apex Court for having directed the Union and the State governments and the University Grants Commission to create environmental awareness among the students and the public. Although the fourth estate has contributed a great deal in highlighting some of the crucial problems of environment, the government on its part has not done enough.[46] All environmental hazards can be attributed to the lack of minimum degree of environmental awarness among the educated elite and the common masses. Even the devastating impact of Bhopal gas tragedy and the Delhi gas leak accidents have not opened the eyes of the government and the universities to incorporate ecological and environmental considerations in planning and development activities and recast the teaching and research programmes at the school, college and university levels. In order to conserve the natural environmental quality and develop human resources that constitute the basic foundation for meaningful economic

growth, people must be educated on crucial topics like pollution, population management, forestry, wild life, health and natural resources conservation through print and electronic media and revised educational curricula. It is hoped that the Central & State Government and the University Grants Commission would move in the right direction to ensure the survival of plant, animal and human population so that there will be no conflict between environment and development.[47]

5. More conditional clearance by expert committees and pollution control boards cannot ensure safety of the environment. Only environmental awarness among the people can make them put up a united fight to protect their own health and environment.[48]

6. The citizens of India should unite and wage a war against pollution and against reckless actions of the Government which is encouraging industrialization without taking into account environmental safeguards.[49]

7. Last but not the least, the suggestion made by the Supreme Court, in 1986, in the 'Delhi Gas Leak' case,[50] for the setting up of environmental courts for speedy disposal of problems relating to health, sanitation, water, air quality and industrial nuisance, if implemented, would be a step in the right direction. At the same time, there is a need to evolve an enlightened public opinion through the movements and struggles launched by those at the receiving end of environmental exploitation.

Wildlife Protection

General

Denotification of forests protected under the Wildlife (Protection) Act, 1972 has become the latest in a list of government actions that openly violate environmental protection laws. It has been evident for some time that the only law that has successfully prevented forests from being encroached upon in the Wildlife (Protection) Act, 1972 (amended in 1991) under which the core areas have to be left without any human incursion to protect endangered plants and animal life. Thus, while forest laws that prohibit dereservation have been routinely violated, no one had touched the sanctuaries. The last action which had taken place in Gujarat[51] and Maharashtra,[52] was disturbing because once industry, or tourist resorts, are allowed to locate in or near protected areas, other transgressions cannot be stopped. This will mean inevitable end of these precious resources which are necessary not only for the survival of wild species of fauna and flora but also replenish water sources and provide food security for future generations by protecting wild genetic materials.

Meanwhile, other environmental controversies such as Sardar Sarovar Project,[53] Bhitarkanika case,[54] the Circus case,[55] the Ridge case,[56] the Narayan Sarovar sanctuary case[57] continue to remain in the public eye.

On a smaller scale are projects like the Konkan Railway and the East Coast Road. In both instances, while the need for roads or railways is not disputed by environmentalists, they have emphasised that even such projects must incorporate environmental and social concerns in the process of planning and design. When this is not done, there is a resistance from local people which in turn leads to delay and constant over-runs.

Denotification and Some of the Provisions of the Wildlife (Protection) Act, 1972

Most of the officials are hell bent on denotifying sanctuaries. They give the reason that the provision of the Wildlife (Protection) Act, 1972 as amended in 1991 do not allow local communities to harvest the forest for their meagre survival, but this is not a fact. The Act provides:

> "... nothing in this Section shall prevent a member of a scheduled tribe; subject to the provisions of Chapter IV, from picking, collecting or possessing in the district he resides any specified plant or part or derivative thereof for his bonafied personal use."[58]

The Act also deals with the declaration of Sanctuaries, National Parks and closed areas, rights of residents, powers of the Collectors etc.[59] The Act also provides the following:

> "the Collector may. . . allow, in consultation with the Chief Wildlife Warden, the continuance of any right of any person in or over any lands within the limits of the sanctuary".[60]

The fact is that the Wildlife Act protects *adivasis* by protecting their forests from commercial exploiter. Any attempt to argue otherwise would be to invite the accusation that the spirit of the wildlife laws of our country are sought to be twisted for ulterior motives.

With Mrs. Indira Gandhi's death, the rot began to creep in. Rajiv Gandhi was never quite as committed to the subject, but he did not allow any erosion of his mother's wildlife protection initiatives to take place. After he (Rajiv Gandhi) died, however, subtle signals from the Prime Minister's office, to the the effect that wildlife was no longer a priority issue, caused the rot to India's wildlife protection initiatives to become well and truly entrenched.

REFERENCES

1. Viegas and Menon, *The Impact of Environmental Degradation on People*, ISI, New Delhi (1989), 7.
2. Gadgil and Vartak, 1974, 314–320, quoted in *Towards A New Forest Policy: People's Rights and Environmental Needs*, Edited by Franandes and Kulkarni, ISI, New Delhi (1989), 84–85.
3. *Ibid.*
4. *Supra* note 1.
5. *Ibid.*
6. Bombay Forest Enquiry Commission, 1887, also see FRI, 1981.
7. Joshi 1985, 47–48, see note 2.
8. Forest Research Institute (FRI) 1981, 330. The new name of FRI is CFRE (Council of Forest Research & Education).
9. Government of India, 1952.
10. The Act came into force on May 1, 1865.
11. Section 1A.
12. FRI, 1981.
13. Constitution Forty-Second Amendment Act, 1976.
14. The Ordinance was issued on 25.10.80 vide No. 17 of 1980.
15. Act no.69 of 1980.
16. S.2 of The Forest (Conservation) Act, 1980.
17. Diwan Paras, *Environment Protection*, Deep & Deep, New Delhi, 1987, 162.
18. Harsh Anshman, *Adivasion Ke Daman Ka Naya Silsila*, *Jansatta* (Hindi daily), New Delhi, 21 January, 1984, quoted *ibid.*
19. Pathak Shankar, Letter to the Editor *Indian Express*, New Delhi, 21 Jan. 1984, quoted *ibid.*
20. Kutty K.G, 'Silent Valley, After the Sounds and Fury', *Indian Express,* New Delhi, 18 Dec. 1983, quoted *ibid.*
21. The Forest Conservation Act, 1980. The Forest Conservation Rules, 1981, The Cattle Trespass Act, 1871, The Wild Life Protection Act, 1972, The Environment Protection Act, 1986, The Water (Prevention and Control of Pollution) Act, 1984, The Air (Prevention and Control of Pollution) Act, 1981 and the Draft Forest Bill, 1980 and Indian Forest Act, 1927.
22. The Orissa Government has enacted a number of legislations. Only a few of those are mentioned here to keep the reader acquaint with the important laws and rules. These are Orissa Forest Act, 1972, Orissa Forest Produce (Control of Trade) Act, 1981, Orissa Protection of Scheduled Castes and Scheduled Tribes (Interest of Trees) Act, 1981, Orissa Preservation of Private Forest Act, 1947, Orissa (Detection, Enquiry and Disposal of Forest Offences) Rules, 1980.
23. Article 48 A of the Constitution of India (added by 42nd Amendment) Act, 1976.
24. (1988)I, SCC 471.
25. Article 47 of the Constitution of India.
26. *Ibid.*
27. If one analyses the role of the Indian judiciary in saving the environmental deterioration, he will find that the judiciary has started taking special cognizance

of the environmental explosion since the year 1980. In 1987 it has reached the highest peak. During this year the Supreme Court (SC) has decided 13 cases whereas different High Courts have decided three cases.

28. Jariwala C.M., *Direction of Environmental Justice in India: Critical Appraisal of 1987 Case Law*, 35 JILI, 1993.
29. *Ibid.*
30. UJ (SC) 1987) (2) 576.
31. *Supra* note 28.
32. *Ibid.*
33. *Ibid.*
34. AIR 1987 SC 1109; see also *Banvasi Seva Ashram* v. *State of UP*, AIR, 1987 SC. 374, the Supreme Court preferred the establishment of thermal power station to general electricity for the protection of forest.
35. *Ibid.*
36. *Ibid.*
37. *Supra* note 31.
38. *Rural Litigation and Entitlement Kendra* v. *U.P.* AIR 1987 SC 359.
39. AIR 1987 AP 171.
40. Rai Usha, *Pressure on Centre to Water Down Forest Act*, Indian Express, Visakhapatnam, 6.8.93, 1.
41. *Ibid.*
42. The Hindu, Visakhapatnam, Sunday, March 26, 1995.
43. The Hindu, Survey of the Environment: 1992, 163.
44. *Supra* note 24.
45. *Supra* note 42.
46. Indian Express, Visakhapatnam 10.8.94, 8.
47. *Ibid.*
48. *Supra* note 46.
49. The Hindu, Survey of the Environment, 1992, 164.
50. *M.C. Mehta* v. *Union of India*, AIR, 1967, 965.
51. The Narayan Sarovar Sanctuary in Gujarat is an important wildlife sanctuary. The same has been denotified and is almost out of existence. The only desert forest in India, is home to the famous and endangered Chinkara deer and a large number of rare species of migratory birds among a host of other important flora and fauna. The exquisite Narayan Sarovar Sanctuary in Gujarat is to be ripped up by limestone mines. . . . almost one third to the Melghat Tiger Reserve has to be sacrificed to big business, large dams and timber contractors . . . .
52. The Radhanagri Bison sanctuary in Maharashtra is being eyed by the Indian Aluminum Company, for the bauxite lying there in . . . . Sariska is being ripped apart by miners who openly share their body with well known politicians and businessmen from New Delhi. The Madhya Pradesh's demand to lower the height of the dam under the Sardar Sarovar Project, in order to cut down on submergence. There is also renewed discussion on the power component of the multi-purpose project and its economic soundness.
53. *Ibid.*
54. The Bhitarkanika sanctuary is situated on the eastern coast of India in the State of Orissa. There exists a beautiful and unique mangrove eco-system which has been notified as Bhitarkanika Wildlife Sanctuary and Gahirmatha National Park. The area is under severe threat due to illegal construction for industrial work and

sponsored tiger prawn farming. These activities are causing immense harm both to the bio-diversity and livelihood of the local fisherfolk.

55. Enslavement and use of animals for entertainment in circuses not only amounts to cruelty to them but also provides an open conduit for loss of endangered wild-life from forests. The supply of circus animals comes from protected areas and the infrastructure for monitoring theft from such areas is grossly inadequate. Some of the best circuses in the world, such as the Russian, the Canadian and the European circuses perform just as well without the use of any animals. The Central Government had issued a notification under Sections 21 and 22 of the Prevention of Cruelty to Animals Act, 1960 whereby training and exhibition of most performing animals was prohibited. The Indian Circus Federation had challenged the Notification in CW No. 890 of 1991 at the Delhi High Court on the grounds that it effected their right to trade and profession and that there was no cruelty in training and exhibiting animals. An interim stay was granted to the Circus Federation permitting the use of animals in circuses. This stay is still in force.
56. The Delhi Ridge, which once upon a time was a glorious forest, has lost its glory due to illegal allotments and deforestation. Historically, the entire Ridge was declared a reserved forest by 1948. The subsequent notifications from 1957 onwards have transferred control over the Ridge to different authorities. In 1980, the Ridge was declared a Protected Forest without prior dereservation which is mandatory under the Forest Act. The Ridge was transferred to the Delhi Development Authority (DDA) in the year 1992 in violation of the Forest Conservation Act, 1980. The 1992 notification transferring the management of the Ridge to DDA was challenged in the Delhi High Court. Consequently, on 24.5.1994, the State Government of Delhi notified the entire Ridge as a "Reserved Forest." Still, violations are there. Today, Ridge is the only catchment area for Delhi's ground water supply and its green lung to keep the air pure and clean.
57. *Infra* note 1.
58. Section 17 A of the Wildlife (Protection) Act, 1972 (amended in 1991).
59. Chapter IV *ibid.*
60. Section 24 C *ibid.*

CHAPTER V

ENVIRONMENTAL JUSTICE IN INDIA

It is observed that the judiciary in India has been taking special cognizance of the environmental pollution from the year 1980. It is not that, prior to 1980, the judiciary neglected the environmental pollution cases, but the gravity of pollution problem was not considered to be serious. The concreted thought and action for keeping the environment free from polllution was realised soon after the Stockholm Conference.[1] Whatever it may be, the judiciary in India, ever since the later part of the 19th century and beginning of 20th century, has inhabitants, but not as environmental pollution cases, rather as cases under Sections 133 and 137 of the Criminal Procedure Code, 1898.[2] Similarly, while interpreting Section 277 of the Indian Penal Code, the Bombay High Court held:

> "Public spring or reservoir did not include under flowing in a continuous stream in a river bed."[3]

So also, the Madhya Pradesh High court in *Babulal* v. *Chanshyamdase*[4] (a case against the officers of a company) held that the Directors and other officials could not be prosecuted unless a specific act or omission was attributed to them or there was *mens rea* on their part. Thus, it became difficult to take the officers of a company to task unless the above was proved.

As mentioned earlier, after realisation of the gravity of pollution, the judicial trend in India has shown a positive signal in deciding the environmental cases. Soon after the Stockholm Conference, the High Courts[5] and the Supreme Court of India decided cases relating to environmental pollution with all precautions. The first noteworthy judgement of the Supreme Court on the subject of environmental pollution was delivered in *Govind Singh* v. *Shanti Sarup*,[6] where a nuisance was caused by the chimney of an oven which was in existence for last 16 or 17 years. The sub-Divisional Magistrate, Khanna ordered for the removal of chimney of the oven, constructed by the baker, as the same was injurious to the health and physical comfort of the people living or working in the proximity of the bakery. On appeal, the Supreme Court upheld the order of the SDM with regard to the removal of the chimney.

This is certainly a right step to preserve environment, free from pollution, in the interest of health, safety and convenience of the public at large.

The Supreme Court of India in *Ratlam Municipality* v. *Vardichand and others*,[7] has taken a remarkable step by construing Section 133 of the Criminal Procedure Code to enable citizens to bring action against the public bodies to force them to be vigilant and to keep the environment unpolluted. In this case, the Supreme Court had to answer the following question:

> "Whether by affirmative action, a court can compel a statutory body to carry out its duty to community by constructing sanitation facilities at great cost and on a time bound basis?"[8]

Krishna Iyer J., while lashing out on the Municipal bodies to make them realise their duty towards sanitation prevent environmental pollution, answered the question in affirmative in the following words:

> "One wonders whether our municipal bodies are functionally irrelevant, baneful rather than boon, and 'lawless' by long neglect, not leader of the people in local self-government."[9]

The Supreme Court also declared the following:

> "Social justice is due to the people and, therefore, the people must be able to trigger off the jurisdiction vested for their benefit in any public functionary like a Magistrate under Section 133 of Cr. P.C."

It is pertinent to note that the Punjab & Haryana High Court decided *Tarsem Singh* [10] and *Ram Lal's*[11] cases keeping aside the guidlines and principles already laid down by the Supreme Court in *Ratlam Municipality*[12] and *Govind Singh* [13] cases.

In both the above cases, the air pollution caused by wheat thrasher and *Panja* (cotton ginning) producing round the clock offensive suffocating dust storms, resulting in serious cough and other skin diseases, was in the scale. In both these cases, the High Court did not dispute the findings recorded by the learned SDM, but based its judgement on the reasoning and principle that the provisions of Section 133 cannot be invoked for a 'long standing nuisance.' In *Tarsam Singh's* case the High Court quashed the SDM's order for the removal of thrasher and *Panja*, whereas in *Ram Singh's* case the learned judge of High Court, after quashing the SDM's order for removal of the thrasher, directed the SDM "to go into the matter of whether the thrasher at the time of the application of the respondent was new or not and may then pass a fresh order."

The above judgements of the Punjab and Haryana High Courts made it clear that installations of thrasher in the instant cases was a public nuisance (causing air pollution) and had it been new one, it could have been removed. In case of old one, it could not be removed.

The above judgement is really a shocking one. It is astonishing as to how the court came to such conclusion in absence of a statutory requirement. Of course some High Courts[14] have taken the same view. It is submitted that such approach of the judiciary is contrary to social justice and misconstruction of Section 133 of the Cr. P.C., whose object is to remove the public nuisance, old or new, to meet the end of justice and achieve the social justice guaranteed by the Constitution of India.[15]

The Bhopal Case

The Bhopal disaster, which took place just after midnight on December 3, 1984, is undoubtedly the worst incident in industrial history. Forty tons of highly toxic methyl isocyanate (MIC), which had been manufactured and stored in Union Carbide's chemical plant in Bhopal, escaped into the atmosphere and killed over 3,500 people who lived in the dispersing chemical's pathway. As many as 200,000 others were injured—many seriously and some permanently. Indeed, the official estimates of death and injury do not convey the enormity of the human tragedy—families and communities disrupted, disabled, dislocated and impoverished.

To ensure that claims arising out of disaster were dealt with speedily, effectively and equitably, the Indian Parliament enacted the Bhopal Gas Leak Disaster (Processing of Claims) Act in March, 1985, known as the Bhopal Act[16] conferred an exclusive right on the Indian Government to represent all claimants both within and outside India, and directed the Government to organise a plan for the registration and processing of the victim's claims.

In April 1986, shortly after the enanctment of the aforesaid Act, the Indian Government used Carbide in the United States. The Government's preference for an American court stemmed from a lack of confidence in its own judicial system, the lure of large damages that an American Jury might award, and the uncertainty about whether carbide would submit to the jurisdiction of an Indian court. The American court, however, declined to try the Bhopal lawsuit, mentioning that India was more appropriate forum. Consequently, in September 1986, nearly two years after the tragedy, the Indian Government sued Carbide in the Court of the District Judge, Bhopal for Rs. 3,900 crores (US$ 3 million) in damages.[16]

The Bhopal case reached the Indian Supreme Court through the separate appeals of Carbide and the Indian Government from the judgement of Justice Seth of the Madhya Pradesh High Court. In April, 1988, Justice Seth awarded interim damages of Rs. 250 crores (US$ 192 million) on the basis of "more than a *prima facie* case having been made out" against the defendants. Carbide's lawyers claimed that the judgement was unsustainable because it amounted to a verdict without trial. The Indian Government appealed because Justice Seth had reduced by 30 per cent District Judge Deo's earlier interim payment award of Rs. 350 crores (US$ 270 million).

Surveying the Bhopal litigation in December 1988, the five judge Supreme Court Bench must have been dismayed at the lack of progress in principal lawsuit. The ineffectiveness of the Indian Government's manoeuvers, combined with Carbide's apparent disregard for the victims, had dimmed the victims' hopes for early compensation. Proceedings in the original lawsuit before the Bhopal District Judge had been stalled. Certain pre-trial matters had yet to be addressed. Four years after the tragedy, the Government had still to finalise its list of authentic claimants.

Rather than proceed rapidly with the trial of the original lawsuit and establish a legal claim on Carbide's American assets with a determinative final judgement, the Government had preferred to pursue a risky shortcut. Encouraged by an early suggestion of Bhopal District Judge Deo, regarding an "interim" award, the Attorney General of India's main litigation stretegy was the pursuit of such a pre-trial award.[17] More than a year had been consumed in appeals since that award. In separate proceedings, additional effort had been spent in a contempt of court action against Carbide, its Chairman and its lawyers. Indeed, there was little in the Government's handling of the Bhopal case that might have impressed the Supreme Court judges with the Government's capacity to devise legal strategies and introduce reformed trial procedures that could bring the Bhopal lawsuit to a swift conclusion.

On February 14, 1989, the Supreme Court induced the Indian Government and Carbide to accept its suggestion for an overall settlement of the claims arising from the Bhopal disaster. Under the settlement, Carbide agreed to pay US$ 470 million to the Indian Government on behalf of all the Bhopal victims in full and final settlement of all past, present and future claims arising from the Bhopal disaster. The entire amount had to be and was paid by March 31, 1989. In addition, to facilitate the settlement, the Supreme Court exercised its extraordinary jurisdiction and terminated all the civil, criminal and contempt of court proceedings that had arisen out of the Bhopal disaster and were pending in subordinate Indian courts.

The Supreme Court of India in December, 1989 in lengthy judgement, upheld the constitutional validity of the Bhopal Act, under which the Indian Government gave itself exclusive right to present Bhopal gas disaster victims in civil litigation against Carbide. The Court acknowledged that the Bhopal Act entitled the victims to give notice and an opportunity to be heard on any proposed settlement, and that the February, 1989 settlement of US$ 470 million failed to give such notice and hearing. Nevertheless, the court concluded that in the special facts and circumstances, the case, "a post-decisional hearing would not be in the ultimate interest of justice." The Court felt that the hearings to be held during the review of the settlement (in review petitions filed by some of the victims in the Supreme Court), afforded a "sufficient opportunity" to the victims. Thus, the court explicitly verified the terms of the settlement. The Court rationalised its view by declaring, 'To do a great right' after all, it is permissible sometimes 'to do a little wrong.'

The Bhopal disaster raised complex legal question about the liability of parent companies for the acts of their subsidiaries, the responsibilities of multinational corporations engaged in hazardous activities, the transfer of hazardous technologies, and the applicable principles of liability.

The Supreme Court on December 1, 1995 in what is known as "Bhopal gas leak disaster-hospital project matter" issued notice to the standing counsel to the Union Carbide Corporation (UCC), a US multinational, to ascertain and inform the Court its response in regard to construction of a hospital in Bhopal with best equipment and infrastructure for the benefit of thousands of gas leak victims suffering due to serious ailment, following the gas disaster the night of December 3 and 4, 1984, keeping in view the humanitarian consideration rather than pure legal aspects (pursuant to Court's order dated October 3, 1991).[17A]

An application from the 'sole trustee' of the trust created by the UCC and its sister concern (for funding the hospital in Bhopal) for suitable diversion of some funds, the Court might consider fit and proper, from out of the 'frozen assets' (of about Rs. 183 crores lying with a Bhopal Criminal Court under 'attachment' in a related criminal case for failure of appearance in Court of some top executives of UCC) was before the Court. This was out of the amount that was realised by the sale of thousands of shares of UCIL held by the UCC (pursuant to Apex Court's orders dated February 14, 1994). The 'trust' is now having a fund of Rs. 125 crores.[17B]

The Chief Justice, Mr. A.M. Ahmadi, Mr. Justice S.P. Bharucha and Mr. Justice S.C. Sen were on the Bench. [17C]

The Apex Court in its judgement delivered on October 3, 1991, in 'Bhopal gas leak review case' *inter alia* ordered the construction of a 500-bed hospital in Bhopal by the UCC and its Indian subsidiary, UCIL for the benefit of thousands of gas victims.[17D]

The Bench, 1st December orders, also asked the trustee (Sir Ian Percival) to place on record the plans and estimates with the certification of the architects and engineers and projection as to the time factor in regard to the construction of the hospital in Bhopal to enable the court to have a clear perscpective of the time likely to be taken and expenditure involved in the construction of the hospital (with 260/500 beds) with supporting infrastructure including operational costs.[17E]

The Bhopal Gas Peeditha Sangharsha Samiti and Bhopal Group of Information and Action Welfare Organisation for Bhopal gas leak victims in their applications moved in this regard submitted that, if the entire 'frozen assets' (Sale proceeds of the shares which were under 'attachment' in related criminal cases before the Bhopal court) were released to the trust, then the concerned 'attachment order' would lose efficacy and force.[17F]

The Bench fixed February 6, 1996, for further hearing of the matter.[17G]

The year 1987 is a memorable year in the judicial history of India as during this year maximum number of environmental pollution cases have been decided by the High Courts and the Supreme Court of India. Not only this, but also, cases on different dimension of the environmental issues have been decided. The following discussion will give an idea about the matter.

The multi-dimensional issues relating to environmental pollution were raised in *M.C. Mehta* v. *Union of India* [18] where the sole question was whether Shriram Food and Fertiliser should be allowed to reopen the caustic chlorine plant. In the instant case, the petitioner had alleged the infringement of right to life of several thousand people due to severe pollution and hazardous activity of Shriram Food and Fertilizer, manufacturing oleum and chlorine situated in the heart of the city of Delhi. The Supreme Court directed the company to take all necessary safety measures before reopening of the plant. There was leakage of chlorine gas from the plant resulting in death of one person and causing hardships to workers and residents of the locality. This was due to the negligence of the management in maintainance and operation of the caustic chlorine plant of the company. The matter was brought before the court through a public interest litigation. The management was directed to deposit a sum of Rs. 20 lakh by way of security for payment of compensation claims of the victims of oleum gas leak with the registrar of the court. In addition, a bank guarantee for a sum of Rs. 15 lakh was also directed to be deposited which shall be encashed in case of any escape of chlorine gas within a period of three years from the date of the judgement, resulting in death or injury to any workman or any person living in the vicinity. Subject to these conditions, the court allowed partial reopening of the plant.[19]

The Shriram Food and Fertiliser case is replete with a number of suggestions to the central government for controlling environmental pollution. For instance, Bhagwati CJ (as he then was) advised the government to set up an ecological science research group consisting of independent professionally trained experts in different branches of science and technology. This group could serve as an information bank for the court and the government departments. Since cases involving issues of environmental pollution, ecological disturbance or destruction and conflict over natural resources were increasingly coming up for adjudication and these cases involved assessment and evaluation of scientific and technical data, there was also an urgent need to set up environmental courts on regional basis, with the professional judges and experts drawn from ecological science research group.[20] The proposals are, no doubt, laudable but until now there seems to be no indication of the willingness of the central government to respond favourably to any of these proposals, leaving the courts with lack of expertise in dealing with the problems involving ecological destruction and environmental pollution. This will leave the courts with no option but to adjudicate upon these issues on the basis of imperfect data gathered from the reports of the committee.

To deal with complaints of environmental excess, the Government proposes to set up a special court with the powers of a High Court, the, then Union Minister of State for Environment and Forest, Mrs. Menaka Gandhi had declared.[21] In view of the same, a bill, seeking to set up a national environment tribunal with benches in different parts of the country was moved in the Lok Sabha on May 24, 1995 to provide relief, and compensation to victims of accidents while handling hazardous substances and for environmental damage.[22]

The Environment Minister, Mr. Kamal Nath, said the tribunal may if it thinks fit, take up cases for claims for compensation *suo moto*. This clause was incorporated in the original bill on the 24th May, 1995 as an official amendment.[23]

The bill was introduced in the Lok Sabha in 1992 during the monsoon session, and also in 1993 monsoon session, and was later referred to a related parliamentary committee.[24]

In the first phase, in addition to the principal bench at Delhi, benches are proposed to be set up in Bombay, Calcutta and Madras. The tribunal will consist of a chairperson, vice-chairperson, judicial and technical members. A bench shall consist of a judicial member and a technical member, Mr. Kamal Nath said.[25]

The tribunal will entertain claims for compensation if it is present within five years from the occurrence of the damage. No other civil court shall have jurisdiction to entertain any claim or action which can be entertained, tried or dealt with by the tribunal.[26]

In *M.C. Mehta's* second case,[27] there were 74 tanneries which discharged their trade effluent, at first into the municipal sewerage and then the waste water joined the river Ganga. A public interest litigation was brought under Article 32 of the Constitution of India to restrict the tanneries from discharging their trade effluent in Ganga till, such time, they put up necessary treatment plants for treating the trade effluent. On behalf of some of the tanneries, it was urged that they would not be able to meet the enormous expenditure on the treatment plant. But the court, rejecting this argument, rightly held that no tannery could be allowed to continue unless it makes provision for the treatment of its trade effluent. The court in this case, it seems, made the treatment plant a part and parcel of the tannery establishment.[28]

The result, in this case was that the tanneries, which had failed to take the minimum stages required for treatment of trade effluents, were ordered by the court to be closed down. Out of 74 tanneries, 37 neither bothered to respond to the notice issued by the court or displayed willingness to take appropriate steps for treatment of trade effluents. If such is the approach of industrialists, the already polluted environment would be more polluted. It is time, that the rigid sanction of law must attract such inaction or casual approach in handling the pollution hazard by those who are not under a constitutional fundamental duty,to protect and improve the natural environment."[29]

In continuation of the previous M.C. Mehta writ petitions, applications were filed by the Delhi Legal Aid and Advice Board and the Delhi Bar Association for award of compensation to those persons who had suffered harm due to the leakage of gas. Initially, these applications came up for hearing before the three judges bench, but in view of the fact that issues involved raised substantial question of law relating to interpretation of Articles 21 and 32, the case was referred to a larger bench of five judges. In the present *M.C. Mehta* case,[30] the Chief Justice, Bhagwati and Justice Oza, out of the previous three judges Bench[31] continued along with Justice Ranganath Misra, Dutta and K.N. Singh. Justice Dutta was the only judge amongst the five judges who had only one opportunity, during the period under review, to sit on the Bench, hearing environmental law cases. Another dimension of this case was that the judgement was delivered by Chief Justice Bhagwati on the eve of his retirement. Though it was the last judgement of the learned Chief Justice, it opened new horizons in the development of environmental law and also administration of environmental justice.[32]

The initial objection of the capitalist for allowing the present writ petition was that neither any claim for compensation was originally made in the writ petition nor was there any amendment made to that effect later on and, as such, the court should not proceed further in the matter. But the Chief justice, brushing aside this plea, held that the enforcement of Article 21 could not be eclipsed by "the hyper technical approach." The judicial zeal to protect the fundamental rights in Article 21 is strengthened further when the court read Article 32 to confer incidental and ancillary powers on it, including, "the power to forge new remedies and fashion new strategies designed to enforce the fundamental rights."[33] This power, according to it, could include, "the power to award compensation in appropriate cases."[34]

One of the preliminary objections raised by the counsel appearing on behalf of *Shriram*, was relating to the *locus standi* of the Delhi Legal and Advice Board and the Delhi Bar Association to move the court. Bhagwati CJ, one of the champions of the "epistolary jurisdiction," endorsed its previous stand that "a public-spirited individual or a social-action group acting *pro bono publico* would suffice to ignite the jurisdiction of this court." The court further allowed two more concessions: *first*, a letter addressed to an individual judge could form part of the writ petition; and *second*, it was not necessary that the letter must be supported by an affidavit. This liberal approach, according to the court, was necessary, otherwise it would frustrate the object and purpose of epistolary jurisdiction. Environmental pollution has very wide dimension of territory and population. It affects both present and future generations. In view of such widespread ramifications, the present stand in the field of environment deserves appreciation.[35]

Although the question, whether *Shriram* case comes within the definition of "the State" under Article 12 of the Constitution engaged attention of the court in all 22 paragraphs of the opinion, the result was that in view of only "four days" to deliver the judgement, the learned Chief Justice held that "this is not a question on which we must make any definite pronoucement at this stage." In spite of this conclusion, if one minutely reads the pronouncement, he will find that at least the Chief Justice was in favour of treating *Shriram* as "the State." It is unfortunate that the strong advocate of liberty jurisprudence had, at the close of his judicial career, to close his wide horizon.[36]

The *M.C. Mehta* case has further opened a new frontier in the Indian jurisprudence. The court discarded the rule laid down in *Rylands* v. *Fletche*[37] and its further developments under the English law. It evolved, what Chief Justice P.N. Bhagwati calls, new principles of strict and absolute liability in the cases of hazardous or inherently dangerous activity resulting in harm to any one. The new principle, according to the court, will not be subjected to the same exception as in the *Rylands* case. Thus, the present *M.C. Mehta* case amends the existing penal provision in the Indian environmental law which recognises the well known exception of "without knowledge" or "exercised due deligence." It may be pointed out that in *M.C. Mehta's* 1st case,[38] the three judges bench consisting of Chief Justice Bhagwati and Justice Madan and Oza exempted "the absolute unlimited liability" in case of, "Act of God . . . of sabotage" but in view of the present opinion, the three judges' order must be read as over-ruled.[39]

This ruling may give a fright to capitalist, but they must not forget that the industry carrying on hazardous and inherently dangerous activity must include in their cost, the expenditure on compensation in events of an accident. Now they shall have to make provision for such expenditure before pocketing the entire profit. The present ruling now makes it mandatory for the industrialists to pay serious attention in conducting their business with the highest standard of safety so as to avoid strict and absolute liability.[40]

In *U.P. Pollution Control Board* v. *Modi Distillery*,[41] there was distillery plant in Modi Nagar of Ghaziabad district in Uttar Pradesh. The plant manufactured industrial alcohol and discharged highly noxious and polluted trade effluents into the Kali river in the process of manufacturing. The Water Board, at first required the distillery to get the consent order of the Board before discharging its waste water, but the plant did not take any notice of this. The Board initiated an action against the plant in the court of the judicial magistrate under the Water (Prevention and Control of Pollution) Act, 1974. Meanwhile, the plant moved the High Court and the High Court gave him protection on the basis of the only flaw in the ill-drafted application by the Board wherein the prosecution was launched against the distillary instead of Modi industries.

The Supreme Court set aside the order of the High Court and held that those who were personally responsible for the conduct of business of the company could be prosecuted and punished under the Act of 1974 inspite of the above infirmity.

In this case the Court did not adopt a too technical approach and thus, caught a big polluter which wanted to escape through a technical but curable error. In fact the capitalist wanted to escape wilfully and deliberately by defying the provision of environmental law. Every citizen is duty bound to protect and improve that natural environment as it is his/her, one of the constitutional obligations.

In *Satish Sabharwal* v. *State of Maharashtra*,[42] an abbatoir, having its plant in the agricultural area, was not permitted to run its business further as it was apprehended that big meat export industry may pollute the river water used by human beings and animals and in no circumstances, should it be permitted to run the plant. Hence, the Supreme Court upheld the order of the High Court with regard to cancellation of permission in the public interest. In this case, the following were the environmental problems that were pointed out:

(i) pollution that could be caused by a large meat export industry:
(ii) use of agricultural land for non-agricultural purposes.

But, no light has been thrown on ecological problems.

The Karnataka High Court in *Chaitanya Pulversing Industry* v. *I.S.P.C. Board*,[43] made a distinction between the prohibitory and remedial measures. The court pointed out that prohibitory orders could be issued in case of those industries which were to be established and are likely to pollute the environment. But in case of established industry, only remedial measure was warranted. The reason of such distinction was that any harsh action against an established industry will affect the livelihood of employees, which may be more hazardous than environmental pollution. Hence, any harsh step of prohibiting the working of the already established factory was not liked by the court. Besides all these considerations, the court has not been lenient towards industrialists. A person without any employment can continue for sometime but living in polluted environment endangers the very life of human beings, animals and plants. In view of the far-reaching dimensions, the unemployment problem cannot be allowed to dominate the ecosystem.

In *M.K. Shrama* v. *Bharat Electronics Ltd.*,[44] the court was petitioned on behalf of the workers of the Bharat Electronics Ltd. (BEL) asking for the compensation for being exposed to the ill-effects of X-ray radiation. No ill effects were found in medical examination but the respondents undertook to pay compensation to affected persons whenever any ill-effects became manifest. The court made various suggestions to prevent such hazards. It also suggested that the officers and workers of the company, who worked within the sensitive portions of the factory, be covered by appropriate insurance cover, over and above the normal insurance, if any, to which as workmen at large, they would have become entitled. Every workman should be insured, additionally to the tune of Rs. 1 lakh and an officer to the tune of Rs. 2 lakhs. The management could also go in for group insurance. The cost of such insurance must be borne by the management. Why should the court ask for an insurance of Rs. 2 lakhs for officers and Rs. 1 lakh for the workers ? Does it mean that human life has different values depending upon the class of the victim? It is a pity that even the pro-poverty Supreme Court could not bury such irrational distinctions, the basis of which was right to property. The common law is replete with instance of such property stratifications for the purpose of determination of rights and obligations.

But, should the Supreme Court of India interpreting the Indian Constitution inherit those colonial biases?[45]

Kisan Sahakari Chini Mills [46] is a case decided by the Allahabad High Court, under water (Prevention and Control of Pollution) Cess Act, 1977.[47] In this case the Uttar Pradesh Board assessed the amount of cess payable by the petitioner for seven years i.e. 1978–85 as Rs. 85,963.50 plus the interest arrears of Rs. 36,926.82 and thus, the total amount payable by the petitioner was Rs. 12,22,890.32. Item no.15, Schedule I of the Cess Act, which was the bone of contention, defined "specified industry" to include "processing of animals or vegetable product industry." The petitioner challenged the assessment order on the ground that sugarcane was neither a vegetable nor a vegetable product and hence, the sugar industry, being not engaged in the processing of any vegetable product, was not covered by the Cess Act. The Allahabad High Court, rejecting this plea, held that the word 'vegetable' should be given a wider amplitude to include sugarcane as well so that the legislative intent did not get lost in bewilderness and as such the sugar industry was subject to cess liability. The High Court further rightly did not accede to the cess avoidance tactic of the mills, for leave to the Supreme Court on the ground that a substantial question of law of general importance was not involved in the present case. In the instant case, there was no big industrialist involved; rather it was *sahakari* unit but still, the approach in the protection of environment had no difference. It is expected at least from the cooperative units to cooperate in the protection of environment.[48]

The sugar industry cannot be denied to be one of the sources of pollution of water and air, it emits foul smell as well. Further, the water polluted by the sugar industries also causes soil pollution. And thus, it cannot avoid the cost of prevention and control of water pollution. In view of wide-ranging pollution activities, it is suggested that the time is ripe for the comprehensive environment pollution cess legislation. This will financially help not only the Water and Air Boards but also other authorities involved in the protection of environment.[49]

In *Banwasi Seva Ashram* v. *State of U.P.*,[50] the question of establishment of a super thermal power industry in a forest area was raised. An area of 1796 acres of forest land was required for the establishment of such industry. The matter, for use of the forest land otherwise, was pending and the court has issued general direction not to dispossess the occupants of the said land. In the meanwhile, the Government of Uttar Pradesh initiated proceedings for acquisition of the above forest area.

The Supreme Court passed an order favouring establishment of the super thermal power plant. The court, in this case, as it seems, went in favour of developmental work, even disfavouring the environmental protection. The court put forth the following views in favour of its decision:

> "long term adverse effects on national economy as also on the living process," yet in view of the fact that India has "suffered a tremendous set back in industrial activity for want of energy," a scheme to generate electricity "cannot be deferred."[51]

Mining activity is a source of environmental pollution. Such operation requires clearing of the dense lush green forest. It affects the flow of the streams, disturbs the natural quiet, and also the soil and the habitat of wild animals, birds, wild tribes, and affects the mountain range. Further, the removal of important minerals affects adversely the self-purifying capacity of rivers. These are some of the many ill-effects of the mining activities on the environment. At the same time, quarrying of the minerals and other deposits is an impregnate ingredient in the development process. If the valuable deposits are not quarried, the country will have to import them from outside, thus involving a huge amount of foreign exchange which is a difficult proposition and thus the mining activities continue. The above scenario raises the complex and difficult question of balancing ecology with development. This difficulty is faced by the government when the Department of Environment, Forest and Wildlife vetoed 32 out of 59 mining projects. Now, coming to the judiciary, in three cases, the Supreme Court was confronted with this difficult task. It was only in one case that the balance tilted in favour of the protection of environment and in the rest of the cases the development process was given priority.[52]

In *Rural Litigation and Entitlement Kendra* v. *U.P.*,[53] the main question before the Apex court was whether the mine lessees could be allowed to mine quarrying operations. The court was confronted with the difficult task of either to protect the ecology and environment or to make available to the country, high grade limestone deposits. The court in the present case shifted its responsibility and preferred a decision by the bureaucrats over the judicial finding.[54] Ranganath Mishra J observed:[55]

> It is for the Government and the Nation and not for the Court, to decide whether the deposit should be exploited at the cost of ecology and environmental considerations of the industrial requirement should be otherwise satisfied.

Such balancing is bound to be influenced by the priorities of the balancing authority and the priorities are determined by a variety of factors, the class interest being most prominent. Even judicial balancing may not be free from class bias. This is obvious from the fact that at the next hearing of the case, the court (Ranganath Mishra and M.E. Dutt JJ) expressed the view that mining operations might be allowed to the extent it was necessary in the interests of the defence of the country as also for safeguarding the foreign exchange position.[56]

Ambika Quarry Works v. *State of Gujarat* [57] is another case where the writ petition entered around the question of how to strike a balance between the need of exploitation of mineral resources lying hidden in the forests and arrest growing envrionmental deterioration. The Supreme Court favoured afforestation in place of quarrying minerals. In this case the government granted lease to the appellants to quarry minerals from certain lands which were dereserved from forest area for a period of ten years. Before the expiry of the said period, the appellants applied for renewal of the said lease. It was rejected by the government because the land fell in the 'reserved forest' area to which the prohibition, under the Forest (Conservation) Act, 1980 applied. Section 2 of this Act provided certain restrictions on the use of forest land for non-forest purposes. The appellants took the plea that once the government dereserved that forest land for non-forest purpose in the year 1971, the restriction under Section 2 would not apply in the present case. The court, rejecting the plea, held that the appellants were asking for renewal of the quarry lease which would lead to further deforestation and this would frustrate the primary purpose of the Act "to prevent further deforestation."[58] Sabyasachi Mukherjee J. distinguished the present case from the facts and circumstances of *Banshi Ram Modi*.[59] In the latter case, the respondents, while carrying on mining operations for mica came across two associate minerals and sought permission for mining these minerals as well. The State government, without complying with the restrictions under Section 2 of the Act, gave permission to the respondents. The main question in this case was whether these restrictions applied in the instant case. The Supreme Court answered the question in the negative. The court took the stand that once the forest area had "broken up and cleared before the commencement of the Act," then the provision of the Forest (Conservation) Act, 1980 would not apply."[60]

Though in both cases the forest area was broken up and cleared before the Act came into force, in view of the concern of the judiciary to protect the environment, the court adopted a distinct approach in the present case. The differential treatment is justified because in the latter case the mining activities would continue only on the 5 acres of the dereserved forest land which was already broken up and cleared; whereas in *Ambika Quarry Works* [61] case, more forest land or dereserved forest land would be broken up and cleared for non-forest purposes after coming into forece of the Act of 1980.[62]

In the present case, the court put ample weight on the statement and objects of the Act of 1980 which stated that "the deforestation was caused on a large scale in the country" resulting in "environmental deterioration" and thereby "caused widespread concern."[63]

Offshoots of the population explosion include new construction and the project activities. Whenever these are undertaken, they spoil the greenery of the place. The green grass, tender plants and big trees are uprooted to give way to the new construction and project activities. This way the ecology of that place is disturbed and in turn the environment is adversely affected.[64] In this regard the Supreme Court and the Hyderabad High Court have decided three cases.[65] These cases have been discussed in Chapter IV (Forest and Wildlife Protection) of this book. Hence, to avoid repetition of the facts, these are not discussed here.

In *L.K Koolwal* v. *State of Rajasthan*,[66] D.L. Mahta J. interpreted Article 51A as conferring a constitutional right to the citizens to approach the courts for the enforcement of the duty cast on the state to protect environment:

> We can call Article 51A ordinarily as the duty of the citizens, but in fact, it is the right of the citizens as it creates the right in favour of the citizen to move the court to see that the State performs its duties faithfully and the obligatory and primary duties are performed in accordance with the laws of the land. Omissions or commissions are brought to the notice of the Court by the citizen and thus Article 51A gives a right to the citizen to move the Court for the enforcement of the duty cast on State, instrumentalities, agencies, departments, and local bodies. . . .[67]

The High Court of Rajasthan has given a new interpretation to a fundamental duty converting it into a fundamental right for the purpose of providing standing to citizen to move the court for enforcement of constitutional duty. In this case, on the above reasoning, the court allowed standing to L.K. Koolwal to file a PIL in the High Court on behalf of the citizens of Jaipur, for a direction to Jaipur Municipal Corporation to clean the city of Jaipur. In pursuance of this, the court appointed a commission to investigate into the matter of sanitation of Jaipur. The report revealed that insanitation in many parts of the city was leading to a slow poisoning and it was adversely affecting the life of the citizens. It directed the Jaipur municipality to remove dirt, filth, etc. within a period of six months and clean the entire city of Jaipur.[68]

The court ruled that maintenance of health, preservation of sanitation and environment fell within the perview of Article 21 of the Constitution of India. The executive have to fulfill this constitutional commitment and it could not be allowed to shirk its responsibility on the ground of paucity of funds.[69]

In *Dr. Shivarao Shanta Ram Wagle (II)* v. *Union of India*,[70] the petitioner moved the High Court of Bombay under Article 226 for a direction to restrain the government from releasing 7,500 cartons of imported Irsih butter as the same was contaminated and was unfit for human consumption. The Irish butter was imported into India under EEC grant-in-aid for operation flood programme for Greater Bombay milk scheme. The court turned down the petition on the ground that it was unsuited to adjudicate upon highly technical matters. It observed that the authorities concerned were fully aware of the problem and the material available from the laboratory tests clearly indicated that there was no contamination by nuclear fallout in the imported butter.[71]

On a special leave petition, following the example of Shriram, the Court appointed a three person expert committee to give its opinion on the question whether milk and dairy products containing man-made radio nuclides within permissible level, were safe and/or harmless for human consumption. The committee reported that such products were safe and harmless.[72]

The court (A.P. Sen and L.M. Sharma JJ) agreed with the conclusion reached by the expert committee and refused to issue directions to the government as prayed by the petitioner. It agreed that it was beyond the judicial function to decide the questions involving scientific complexities.[73]

The main controversy in the *Doon Valley* case had been as to whether for social safety and for creating hazardless environment for the people to live in, the mining in the area should be permitted or stopped. In its judgement, dated 30 August, 1988,[74] the Supreme Court had given direction to totally stop the operation of mining in certain areas on the ground of environmental protection. The court had, however, allowed the mine, in lease no. 99, to continue mining till the original lease expired in 1990. In *R.L.E. Kendra* v. *State of U.P.*,[75] a petition was moved praying the Supreme Court to modify its earlier judgement and direct the closing of mine in lease no. 99 also. On reconsideration of the matter, the court found that the mine in question was similarly situated i.e. lying within the municipal limits of Mussoorie and should, therefore, be closed.[76]

Environmental control once again became the subject-matter of PIL. In *Mukti Sangarsh Movement* v. *State of Maharashtra*,[77] a PIL was initiated to prevent reckless exploitation of a Kerala river running through some parts of Maharashtra and ultimately joining river Krishna. Since the exploitation of sand of the river was adversely affecting its bed, the petitioners asked the Supreme Court for a direction for stopping of commercial quarrying of sand and for regulating excavation and other activities connected with commercial exploitation of sand keeping in view the safety of the river-bed and the adjoining areas.[78]

A committee of experts appointed by the Government of Maharashtra suggested that the exploitation of sand from the river should be minimised and suitable sites for sand excavation should be identified and exploitation should be confined to such sites only. The committee also recommended for the framing of a set of rules for regulating the exploitation so as to prevent environmental degradation.[79]

The court declined to intervene in view of the care taken by the committee and the approach adopted by the Government of Maharashtra in following the guidelines framed by the expert committee.[80]

In *F.K. Hussain* v. *Union of India*,[81] a PIL alleged violation of right to potable water, by large scale withdrawal of water from wells by electric pumps by the local administration of Lakshadeep Islands. It was stated in the petition that ground water resources were limited and potable water was in short supply in the islands and therefore, large withdrawal of water by electric pumps was depleting the water resources and this amounted to an invasion of right to life.[82]

The Court held that right to sweet water and right to free air were attributes of right to life, for these were the basic elements which sustained life itself. Since, potable water was in short supply in Lakshadeep, the administration could not be allowed to go ahead with the scheme of digging wells by electric pumps. The local administration was, therefore, directed to evolve safeguards to stop withdrawal of ground water at a cut-off level, to impose restrictions and introduce a system of effective monitoring at all levels so that over-exploitation of water resources were contained.[83]

The Rio Declaration of June 1992, proposing a long list of environmental measures for 21st century, if taken seriously, will go long way in protecting the atmosphere, the forests, flora and fauna and in ensuring safe and clean technology. In this Earth Summit, environmentalists from all over the world emphasised the need to cultivate enrironmental friendly habits among the people. At the summit, B.B. Ghali, the U.N. Secretary-General mooted the "Polluter Pays" principle and blamed the rich nations for harming the environment of the poor and developing countries. On the eve of the summit, the Delhi traffic police was seen with gas masks to shock the Delhites and make them aware of the dangers of vehicular pollution.[84]

The court-recourse to prevent vehicular pollution in Delhi has been an important event of the year 1991. In *M.C. Mehta* v. *Union of India*,[85] a PIL was brought before the Supreme Court to prevent vehicular pollution in Delhi, caused by increasing number of petrol and diesel driven vehicles. A Bench comprising Ranganath Misra, CJ, M.N. Venkatachalaih and A.M. Ahmadi JJ held the Delhi administration responsible for growing vehicular pollution in Delhi. The court directed the Delhi administration to place before it, a complete list of the prosecution launched against the vehicles, for causing pollution by infringing of various requirements of the law with particular reference to the vehicles, nature of the vehicles, dates of prosecution and the nature of the offences for which prosecution has been launched and results, if any, of such prosecutions from 1.4.1990. The particulars of vehicles, registration of which have been suspended, had also to be provided to the court.[86]

The court advised the Ministry of Environment to carry out appropriate experiment with the device brought out by the National Environmental Engineering Research Institute, Nagpur for reducing pollution. The court directed that steps be taken by the government that every vehicle to be manufactured after 1.4.1990 or 1.7.1990 should have the aforesaid device as an in-built mechanism to reduce pollution. The operating vehicles were also expected to adopt the same pollution reducing device, the court said.[87]

According to Ashish Kolhar, an environmentalist, the major pollutant in Delhi is vehicular emissions, responsible for sixty per cent air pollution. About one thousand tones of pollutants are released by two million odd vehicles in Delhi. In other countries the burden of pollution control is on the manufacturers of vehicles. The Supreme Court has, therefore, made a welcome endeavour to see that only environmental friendly vehicles are manufactured. It is respectfully submitted that like in other countries, India should also have a comprehensive legislation placing the burden of pollution control on the manufactures of vehicles.[88]

In another PIL matter *M.C. Mehta* v. *Union of India*,[89] the Supreme Court was asked to issue directions for closing down hazardous industries located in the densely populated areas of Delhi and for regulating the air pollution caused by automobiles operating in Delhi and also by thermal units generating power for Delhi Electric Supply Undertaking (DESU). The Court (Ranganath Misra CJ, M.H. Kania and Kuldip Singh JJ) pointed out the lack of vision and inadequate statesmanship which allowed many of the industries in Delhi to grow perilously close to human habitation. Hindustan Insecticides Limited was one of the industries which had made the industrial belt, a part of the city. DESU had three generating units located in densely populated arcas. Delhi Transport Corporation remained one of the most notorious polluting agencies.[90]

The judges referred to the report of the monitoring committee according to which, as on 31.3.1982, Delhi had a total number of 5, 92, 58 vehicles. The vehicular population grew to about 14 lakh in 1990. Every year one lakh vehicles were increasing in Delhi.[91]

What could the Supreme Court do in this matter? Apparently it could do no more than pass stricutres against the Delhi Administration for failing to prevent vehicular pollution. Another standard device with the court has been to appoint a committee to look into the matter. Accordingly the government was directed to set up a high powered committee by 18.3.1991 with K.N. Saikia J as Chiarman and M.C. Mehta, N.S. Tiwana and S.G. Shah as members. The committee was asked to (a) make an assessment of the technologies available for vehicular pollution control in the world; (b) make an assessment of the current status of technology available in India for controlling vehicular pollution; (c) look at the low-cost alternative for operating vehicles at reduced pollution levels in the metropolitan cities of India; (d) examine the feasibility of measures to reduce/eliminate pollution from motor vehicles both in short-term and long-term basis and make appropriate recommendations in this regard: and (e) make specific recommendations on the administrative/legal regulations, required for implementing the recommendations.[92]

The court agreed that law alone could not help in restoring a balance in the biosphere disturbance. Only a sustained effort and result-oriented strategic action could do the needful to make people aware of the hazards of vehicular pollution.[93]

Subhas Kumar v. *State of Bihar* [94] is an example of abuse of PIL, for satisfying personal grudge or enmity rather than for preventing environmental degradation. In this case one Subhas Kumar asked for a direction, directing Director of Collieries, West Bokaro Collieries (WBC) at Ghatotand, District Hazaribagh, Bihar, and Tata Iron and Steel Company Limited (TISCO) to stop forthwith discharge of slurry/sludge from its washeries at Ghatotand into Bokaro river. It was discovered by the court that the petitioner, an influential businessman had been purchasing slurry from TISCO and WBC for the last seven years but when they refused to succumb to the pressure of the petitioner for supplying more quantity of slury, he removed the company's slurry in an unauthorised manner and also initiated several proceedings against the company before the Patna High Court. There was intrinsic evidence that the primary purpose of filing PIL was not to serve any 'public interest.' Instead, it was in self-interest, the sole purpose of the petitioner being to collect the slurry and transport the same for his business purposes.[95]

Rejecting the petition K.N. Singh J remarked.

> A petition under Article 32 for the prevention of pollution is maintainable at the instance of a person or even by a group of social workers or journalists. But recourse to proceedings under Article 32 of the Constitution should be taken by a person genuinely interested in the protection of society on behalf of the community. Public interest litigation cannot be invoked by a person or body of persons to satisfy his or its personal grudge or enmity.[96]

The judge then added:

> Public interest litigation contemplates legal proceedings for the vidication or enforcement of fundamental rights of a group of persons or community which are not able to enforce their fundamental rights on account of their incapacity or poverty or ignorance of law.[97]

In *Bangalore Medical Trust* v. *B.S. Mudappa,*[98] public interest action was utilised to assert people's right to open space for recreation, fresh air, play ground for children and other conveniences and amenities. Here, the resident of a locality challenged the action of Bangalore Development Authority (BDA) converting an open space reserved for park into a hospital site in favour of a private body. A Division Bench of the Karanataka High court allowed the petition. The Supreme Court confirmed the judgement of the High Court holding that the order of the state government to convert the site reserved for public park into a civic amenity and to allot it to a private nursing home was null and void. On discovering that Supreme Court characterised this action of the chief minister as a breach of public trust.[99] In a concurrent opinion Thommen J observed:

> Protection of environment, open space for recreation and fresh air, play ground for children, promenade for the residents or amenities are matters of great public concern and of vital interest to be taken care of in a developmental scheme . . . . The public interest in the reservation and preservation of open space for parks and play ground cannot be sacrificed by leasing or selling such sites to private persons for conversion for some other user.[100]

In *Dhanu Taluka Environment Protection Group* v. *Bombay Suburban Electric Supply Company Limited*,[101] a PIL was filed before the Bombay High Court, against setting up of a public project involving environmental pollution problem. The petitioners had challenged the clearance given by the state government to the proposal of Bombay Suburban Electric Supply company for construction of a thermal power plant at a place near Bombay. The High Court dismissed the petition as the government was found to have exercised its power in proper manner looking into all aspects of environmental problems. The Supreme Court (S. Ranganathan, S.C. Agrawal and N.D. Ojha JJ) agreed with the High Court and held that it was "primarily for the government concerned to consider the importance of public projects for the improvement of social and ecological balance, avoidance of deforestation and maintenance of purity of the atmosphere and water free from pollution in the light of various factual, technical and other aspects that may be brought before its notice, by various bodies of laymen experts and public workers. It must strike a just balance between the two competing objectives.[102]

The *Doon Valley* [103] case initiated in 1985 is still on the file of the Supreme Court. On 30.8.1988, by a decision of the court,[104] an exception was made in the case on mining lease no. 99, since its period was to expire in 1990. The lessee was given the benefit of carrying on the operations as an exceptional case, on certain conditions on the basis of representations made and undertaking given before the court by the lessee. Later, the representations were found to be incorrect and mining in the lease in question was also directed to be stopped with effect from

31.12.1988, but the lessee was allowed to remove limestone already collected before that date.[105]

The monitoring committee appointed by the Supreme Court to supervise the afforestation programme undertaken by the lessee reported that the conditions laid down by the court were not being honoured by the lessee. The report also indicated that instead of honouring its undertaking and complying with the judicial directions, the lessee had surreptitiously been indulging in fresh mining operations damaging the area and the environment. In *R.L. & E. Kendra* v. *State of U.P.*,[106] the Supreme Court constigated the lessee for making a false representation and doing nothing from 30.8.1988 till 31.12.1988 to reforest the land. The court, therefore, directed that the activities of the lessee be stopped and he be compelled to pay a sum of Rs. 3 lakhs to the fund of the monitoring committee by June 1991.[107]

Undoubtedly, the PIL activism has, to a limited extent, enhanced the judicial intervention in the prevention of environmental pollution. Every major PIL opinion or order is attracting wide media attention. For instance, the orders issued by Kuldip Singh and K. Ramaswamy JJ on 15.5.1992 for the closure of all mechanical stone crushers in Delhi and Faridabad received detailed coverage in all leading newspapers followed by the critiques of the court order both by experts and social activists. In this order, the judges passed stricutures against Delhi Development Authority (DDA), Delhi Municipal Corporation (DMC) and Central Pollution Control Board (CPCB) for being wholly remiss in the performance of their statutory duties in preventing environmental pollution in Delhi. The court noted that all the stone crushers are emitting hazardous dust round the clock. They were ordered to be closed with immediate effect if they did not have certificates from CPCB.[108]

Soon after the aforesaid order was reported in newspapers, more details were made available. Of the 21 directions issued in *Bandhua Mukti* on 16.12.1983, one related to stone crushers emitting hazardous dust must either instal dust sucking machines or arrange for water sprinklers to ensure that the lethal fine dust did not fly in the air and if the stone crushers did not comply with judicial directions, they had to be banned.[109]

Obviously, these stone crushers defied court orders ever since 1983. It is submitted that even the stricutures passed by the Supreme Court against DDA, DMC and CPCB would be meaningless, because these strictures are general in nature and are not specifically directed against any one official or department responsible for continued pollution.[110]

In *M.C. Mehta* v. *Union of India,* [111] a PIL succeeded in getting a favourable opinion from the Supreme Court for educating the people about the hazards of environmental pollution. The judges agreed that law alone could not be an effective instrument for protecting environment unless there was an element of social pressure or social acceptance and the interaction was voluntary. The court directed the central and state governments to exhibit slides containing information and messages on environment in cinema halls, spread of related information through radio and television, and making environment a compulsory subject in schools and colleges. These messages were to be designed to educate the people about their social obligation in the matter of the upkeep of the environment in proper shape and making them alive to their obligation to ensure that they do not act as polluting agencies or factors. The court also directed the authorities to invariably enforce, as a condition of license of all cinema halls, touring cinemas and video parlours, to exhibit free of cost, at least two slides messages on environment in each show undertaken by them. The Ministry of Environment was directed to prepare slides carrying the message home, on various aspects of environment and pollution. Licenses were to be cancelled if a cinema hall failed to exhibit these slides. The Ministry of Information and Broadcasting was also directed to start the production of information films of short duration. The programme controlling authorities of the Doordarshan (Television) and All India Radio were directed to take proper steps to make interesting programmes and broadcast the same on radio and television. All directions issued by the court had to be complied with from 1.2.1992.[112]

The court also advised the University Grants Commission to consider the feasibility of making environment a compulsory subject at every level of college education.[113]

V. Lakshmipathy v. *State of Karnataka*,[114] underlines the importance of governmental accountability in protecting environment. The Karnataka High Court warned that "when the administrators do not mend their ways, the courts become the battleground of social upheaval" and "if the administrators show indifference to the principle of accountability, law will become a dead-letter on the statute book and public interest will be casualty."[115]

In this case the petitioners had embarked upon PIL to prevent the state government from allowing an earmarked residential area to be used for industrial purposes. It was alleged that in gross violation of the Karnataka Town and Country Planning Act, 1961 the government had allowed running of factories, workshops, factory sheds, manufacture of greases and lubricating oils by distillation process and also production of inflammable products. Agreeing with the petitioner, the court ruled that all the licenses, permissions and certificates of change of land-use, issued by the administrators to various industry owners were illegal, void and violative of Article 21 of the Constitution. Acknowledging the entitlement of clean environment as a basic human right incorporated in Article 51A(g) of the Constitution, the court remarked.[116]

> The right to life inherent in Article 21 . . . does not fall short of the requirements of qualitative life which is possible only in an environment of quality. Where, on account of human agencies, the quality of air and the quality of environment are threatened or affected, the Court would not hesitate to use its innovative power within its epistolary jurisdiction to enforce and safeguard the right to life to promote public interest.

Lakshmipathy is notable for its elaborate discussion on the hazards of environmental pollution. The court took the view that the movement for restoration and maintenance of a livable environment required curbing the power of narrowly-oriented administrative agencies in the appropriation of the dwindling acreage of land and water not already irrevocably appropriated.[117]

Therefore, the real problem was rendering "big Government more responsive to the needs of the individuals whom it governs."[118] The State and society owed an onerous obligation to posterity to clean air, clean water, greenery and open spaces and these ought to be elevated to the birth rights of every citizen. The court further observed that the fundamental duties enshrined in the Constitution were intended to promote people's participation in restructuring, reshaping and building a welfare society. Hence, protection of environment was a constitutional priority, the neglect of which would only invite disaster. Article 226 enables the citizens to move the High Court to enforce the performance of statutory obligations of any authority coming within the sweep of Article 21, namely under anti-pollution laws.[119]

However, in *K.K. Vasant* v. *State of karnataka*,[120] the Karanataka High Court spelled out the limits of judicial action in environmental litigation. In this case, PIL was brought for directions to the state government to declare the forest of many catchment areas as virgin forest, not to be subjected to any exploitation in any way. Further, directions were sought to amend the Forest Act, 1963 to express the intent of the legislature in the preamble and strict execution of the same to cancel licence and permits of the established forest based industries whose products for the consumers had substitutes in the nature of metals, iron, steel, aluminium, cotton etc. The petitioners also requested the court to issue directions to the state government to protect, preserve and conserve the rich flora and fauna and other medicinal plants in all forests and to restrain from spending revenue on expansive advertisements and divert the same for afforestation projects by proper implementation.[121]

Relying on Ryral Litigation[122] and Shimla Medical College,[123] the Karnataka High Court declined to issue directions as prayed for, by the petitioners. The court concluded that in a scheme of separation of powers envisaged by the founding fathers, it was impermissible for the judiciary to interfere with the daily routine administration of the state or in the making of laws by the legislature. Judicial review was meant to protect basic human and fundamental freedom but when it came to matter of policy or law-making, the court had no role whatsoever to play. PIL could not allowed to be used for judicial interference upon the spheres reserved by the Constitution to the legislature and the executive.[124]

Goa Foundation v. *Konkan Railway*,[125] emphasises the need to maintain a balance between development and environmental pollution. In this case, a public interest petition was filed by a society to stall a project undertaken by the central government for public benefit. The project involved the laying of new broad gauge railway line passing through the States of Maharashtra, Goa, Karnataka and Kerala. The Konkan Railway Corporation Ltd., a public limited company was set up to fulfil the dreams of the people residing in the west coast by providing a broad gauge railway line from Bombay to Mangalore and then to Kerala. The petitioners prayed that the corporation should be compelled to procure environment clearance for the alignment passing through the States of Goa, from the Ministry of Environment and Forests, Government of India and until such clearance was secured, all the work in respect of providing railway lines should be withheld.[126]

The court declined to interfere with the project of such magnitude undertaken for meeting the aspirations of the people. It was clarified that while examining the gravity of possible adverse effects on environment, the benefit of which will be derived by large number of people by the construction of rail line could not be brushed aside. According to the court, the project was undertaken only after the approval of renowned experts from the area and the prior approval of central government under Section 2 of the Forest (Conservation) Act, 1980 was not necessary. PIL could not be used for subserving the private interest or the interest of a local area to the detriment of the public at large, the court added.[126A]

In *M.C. Mehta* v. *State of Orissa*,[127] the High Court of Orissa described Articles 48A and 51A as laying down the foundation for the jurisprudence of environmental protection obligating the state and the citizens alike to protect and improve the environment including forests, lakes, rivers, wildlife and to have a compassion for living creatures. In this case, allegations were made against Municipal Committee and S.C.B. Medical College, Cuttack, for causing water pollution by discharge of sewerage from medical college campus and by storm water drain as a result of which thousands of innocent people living in Cuttack and adjacent areas were suffering from water pollution, in violation of right to life guaranteed by Article 21 and the Water (Prevention and Control of Pollution) Act, 1974.[128]

The court examined a survey report submitted by the State Pollution Control Board and found that untold health injuries were caused to the people by the use of water. The authorities were found to be indifferent and callous towards the magnitude of the problem caused by water pollution. The court referred to the report of the World Health Organisation which indicated that one hospital bed out of four in the world was occupied by a patient who was ill because of water pollution.[129]

The court directed the concerned branches of the state government to take immediate steps to prevent and control water pollution in the affected areas and to constitute a committee to consider the reports and take necessary steps to maintain wholesomeness of water which was supplied for human consumption.[130]

The editorial column of the Hindustan Times, New Delhi (ed) dated 18.8.1993, has very rightly pointed out that the judicial efforts to control pollution have not so far shown any positive gains. For instance, the Supreme Court had ordered the closure of 25 units situated on the banks of Ganga for not conforming to pollution laws. Instead of setting up effluent treatment plant as directed by the court, these units were found to have been merrily carrying on their pollution activities as usual, compelling the Apex court to think in terms of initiating contempt proceedings.[131]

It is quite clear that despite various anti-pollution laws, there has been very few instances of closure of polluting agencies. The main reason is that the state pollution control boards are hamstrung by the lack of infrastructural facilities to deal with the situation. In addition to this, political pressure also deter the boards from taking action against erring units.[132]

General Public of Saproon Valley v. *State of H.P.*,[133] came before the High Court of Himachal Pradesh as a public interest litigation. In the instant case, it was allged that mining of limestone in the Saproon valley caused great damage to the fields below, the environment and it leads to pollution of water and soil erosion of surrounding land and ecological imbalance. The reports made to the Court were found to be contradicting each other and it was on that account that, eventually, the Committee, with Secretary (Industries) to the Government of Himachal Pradesh, as Chairman, was directed to be constituted to make an in-depth study of the problem. This Committee, as detailed earlier, included exports like the Director of Geological Survey of India, of Mines Safety and Professors of Forestry and Geology. The Committee drew up a detailed report. It set before itself certain guidelines and then proceeded to classify the mines into two categories A and B. The Committee observed that mines in Category B should be stopped. The lessees of said mines pleaded that Category B mincs also deserved to be permitted to work irrespective of the recommendations of the Committee appointed by the High Court and further, that the total stoppage of mining operations in the Saproon area was not called for. They also canvassed that curative steps to protect the environments could be taken without stopping the mining.[134]

In the present case, High Court's appointment of an expert committee was considered to be the best way for ascertaining necessary facts. It was further held that committee consisted of responsible persons whose bonafides could neither be nor has been assailed, therefore, the recommendations of the committee should be given effect. The court further directed constant supervision of the mining operation and permitted mines of Category A to continue, in terms of the recommendations made by the committee.[135]

In *People United for Better Living in Calcutta* v. *State of W.B.*[136] the question came before the court to strike a balance between environment and development programme. While it is true that in a developing country there shall have to be developments, but that development shall have to be in closest possible harmony with the environment, as otherwise, there would be development but no environment, which would result in total devastation, which, however, may not be felt in present day, but at some future point of time, and then, it would be too late in the day, however, to control and improve the environment. There shall have to be a proper balance between the development and the environment so that both can co-exist without affecting the other.

The court further held:[137]

> Law Courts have a social duty since it is a part of the society and as such, must always function with due regard to the present day problems which the society faces. It is now a well-settled principle of law that socio-economic condition of the country cannot be ignored by a court of law. It is now well settled principle of law that while dealing with matter, the social problems shall have to be dealt with in the way and in the manner it calls for, since benefit to the society ought to be the prime consideration of the Law Courts and ecological imbalance being a social problem ought to be decided by a court of law so that the society may thrive and prosper without any affliction.

Setyavani v. *A.P. Pollution Control Board,*[138] came before the Andhra Pradesh High Court in shape of PIL. The petitioner claimed for an injunction restraining the respondents from making any type of killing of animals, for any purpose and to set aside the industrial license granted in November, 1992 by the Union Government. The next issue of the case related to environmental pollution.

The court referring to the observation of the Supreme Court in *State of Himachal Pradesh* v. *Student's Parent, Medical College, Shimla*[139] held:[140]

> Public interest litigation is a weapon which has to be sued with great care and circumspection and the judiciary has to be extremely careful to see that under the guise of redressing a public grievance, it does not encroach upon the sphere reserved by the Constitution to the Executive and the Legislature.

Further the court referring to the observations of the apex court in *Subhas Kumar* v. *State of Bihar*[141] held:

> Wherein it was observed that public interest litigation cannot be invoked by person or group of persons to satisfy his or its personal grudge and enmity. We also add that public interest litigation cannot be invoked by persons or body of persons to vindicate their sentiments. Therefore, we are of the view that the petitioners are not entitled to approach this court for relief to vindicate their sentimental objections to the industry in a public interest litigation.[142]

The court dismissed the writ petition holding that no substantial question of law, of public importance was involved.

In *Murali Purusothaman* v. *Union of India*,[142] a petition was filed before the Kerala High Court for espousing a public cause of great importance. The petitioner has focused the attention on the consequences of air pollution created through uncontrolled and unmitigated automobiles spitting and hence, prayed for appropriate direction to be issued to the officials concerned for enforcing the statutory measures to reduce the gravity of the problems.

Praising the petitioner for bringing most important problems to the notice of the court, the court held:[143]

> Human life is far more important than vehicular traffic. "Rules are for men and not men are for rules." It assumed contemporary relevance, particularly in the area of environmental cleanliness. No authority, not even the State can be permitted to bide time without enforcing whatever provision is available and without exercising whatever power is commendable to protect human life.

In view of the above, the court issued direction to the State government to take all safety measures immediately.

Executive Engineer Attappady Valley Irrigation Project, Agali v. *Environmental and Ecological Protection Samithy, Agali*,[144] is a case wherein a writ petition under PIL was filed before the court prohibiting contractor from cutting bamboo in forest. Like previous case, in this case, an expert committee was appointed. The report of the committee was found to be defective as no findings were given regarding relevant questions. The matter was remitted back to the Government for decision in the light of further expert opinion and to work out equities in favour of contractor who had spent huge amount in cutting bamboo.

Reversing the decision of the single judge, the court held;[145]

> Environmental protection cases coming under the class of public interest litigation must be handled carefully by the court, both at the stage of granting interim orders and final judgement.

In *Kholamuhana Pry. Fishermen Co-operative Society* v. *State* [146] the question before the court was Article 21 of the Constitution—right to life, which includes right to enjoyment of pollution free atmosphere. The second question was with regard to classification of fisheries as "capture" and "culture". The court held the classification to be reasonable and not arbitrary. The non-fishermen cannot be discriminated against under changed circumstances. However, under the policy, great harm to the ecology to be caused by massive adoption of extensive and intrusive prawn culture for earning revenue by way of "prawn dollar" like "petro-dollar" was not entertained by the Court. The Court instead of quashing policy, directed its prunning, trimming and dressing to make it reasonable regarding conferment of right on non-fisherman and to subserve public interest and also for maintenance of pollution-free environment.

In *Animal Feeds Dairies and Chemicals Ltd.* v. *Orissa State*,[147] the petitioner had set up a factory in 1975 for manufacture of cattle and poultry feed in village Jharpada within the Municipal limits of Bhubaneswar. On 8.7.1986, the Government of Orissa issued notification in exercise of the powers conferred by the Air Pollution Act, 1981 declaring the areas and premises of the industry coming under the air pollution control areas.

After examining several questions, the court came to the conclusion that it is a fact, the area where the petitioner's factory is situated, comes under the air pollution control area, but there was a possibility of emission of foul odour itself without a finding, that there has been emission of air pollutant, would not clothe the jurisdiction with the Board to issue any direction. In the absence of any finding that the petitioner's factory emits any air pollutant as defined in Section 2(a) of the Act it was not within the jurisdiction of the Board to issue the direction to shift or close down the industry in exercise of powers under Section 31A of the Act. The action of the Board must be held to be without jurisdiction and therefore it is quashed.[148]

On March 9, 1995, the Supreme Court, while modifying its earlier order made in December'94 in "Costal Zone Regulation 1991 notification implementation case," directed that all the restrictions and prohibitions regarding construction and setting up of industries or for any other purpose, contained in the notification dated February 19,1991, issued by the Union Ministry of Environment and Forest "shall be meticulously followed by all the concerned states" (namely coastal state concerned including, Tamil Nadu, Pondicherry, Andhra Pradesh, Kerala, West Bengal, Orissa, Gujarat and Maharashtra.[149]

The Feburary, 1991 notification was issued under relevant provision of Sub-rule 3 of Rule 5 of Environment (Protection) Rules, 1986.[150]

In December last, the court in its interim orders, directed that no industrial or construction activity be carried on within 500 meters of high tide lines in all coastal States and Union Territories.[151]

The Bench consisting of Mr. Justice Kuldip Singh and Mr. Justice B.L. Hansaria in its orders, also said that "the activities which have been declared as prohibited within the coastal regulation zone shall not be undertaken" by any of the costal states and Union Territories concerned (respondent States).[152]

The Bench, however, made it clear that "the regulations of permissible activities shall also be meticulously followed."

The restrictions imposed by the Coastal Areas Classification and Development Regulations, contained in Annexture 1 to the February, 1991 notification "shall also be strictly followed by the respondent States," the Bench ordered.[153]

The Bench made these orders in connection with the hearing of pleas from Mr. M.C. Mehta for Indian Council for Enviro-legal Action for enforcing the Union Government's February 1991 notification and also for directions to formulate "Coastal Zone Management Plan" and identify "coastal zone regulation areas" as per the notification in the context of setting up of any industries or any kind of construction activity in the areas concerned. The Bench also issued notice to the Union Ministry of Environment and Forests and also to the State of Goa to file within two weeks their affidavits.[154]

The Supreme Court on May 1, 1995 directed immediate closure of 59 tanneries situated in North Arcot (Ambedkar district, Tamil Nadu) for having not put the required effluent treatment plants despite repeated opportunities given to them earlier by the court and also individual notices issued to them by the Tamil Nadu Pollution Control Board. [154A]

The bench consisting of Mr. Justice Kuldip Singh and Mr. Justice N. Venkatachalya also directed the district authorities to ensure strict compliance with the court's orders.[154B]

The Bench also directed the remaining 496 tanneries in the district (out of a total of 553) to set up either common or individual effluent treatment plants and ensure their effective functioning within three months. Otherwise, these 496 would be liable to be closed down and also be subjected to payment of 'pollution fine.'[154C]

The State Pollution Control Board was asked to give individual notices and also public notice in this regard.[154D]

A Public Interest Litigation (PIL) petition from the Vellor Citizen Welfare Forum was before the Bench.[154E]

According to Mr. M.C. Mehta, who appeared for the petitioner-forum, the pollution caused by these tanneries was so intense that it affected not only the fertility of large areas of agricultural land in the region but also the ground-water table in the area. The acute drinking water problem, because of pollution in the area was also brought to the notice of the International Water Tribunal at Amsterdam, according to counsel.[154F]

On a plea by Mr. R. Mohan, senior advocate for the State Pollution Control Board (SPCB), the Bench stayed further proceedings in the Madras High Court, in the pending writ petitions from 24 tanneries of the region challenging certain notices issued to them by the SPCB for initiating punitive action for setting up the required effluent treatment plants.[154G]

The Supreme Court has on May 9, 1995 directed that no part of the agricultural land in the coastal states of Andhra Pradesh, Tamil Nadu and Pondicherry be converted into commercial aquaculture farms hereafter. No commercial acquaculture farm will be permitted to be set up in these areas.[155]

The Court also ordered that no ground water should be drawn from acquaculture, either for the existing complexes or for those to be set up in future. The State Government have been asked to provide free access to the coastal area to fishermen and tourists.[156]

On a plea from Mr. M.C. Mehta, counsel for the petitioners, and Bench comprising Mr. Justice Kuldip Singh and Mr. Justice Nanavati, asked the State Governments to lock into the problems of the villagers concerned for drinking water and find out whether it would be possible to supply water in tankers to the villages affected.[157]

The District Collectors and the State Governments have been directed to ensure that Court's orders are complied with.[158]

Noted Gandhian Mr. S. Jagannathanan and an organisation 'PREPARE' had in their Public Interest Litigation (PIL) writ petition sought Court's directive to the Union of India and all the coastal States to set up 'coastal management authority' and not to permit intensive and semi-intensive prawn farming in the coastal areas concerned. The petitioners also prayed the court, not to permit Government waste land to be used for prawn culture and to remove the existing encroachments.[159]

Mr. Mehta said that owing to large scale aquaculture in the areas, large scale displacement of poor and traditional fishermen had taken place, affecting their right to livelihood. Even drinking facilities had been depleted in the areas, he pleaded.[160]

Following the Apex Court's earlier orders, a team of scientists from the National Environmental Engineering Research Institute (NEERI), which visited the ecologically fragile areas in the States of Tamil Nadu, Andhra Pradesh and Pondicherry, had since submitted its report to the Court. According to the report from the NEERI, acquaculture units in these areas were, situated within 500 meters of the high-tide lines of the sea, not being in consonance with a notification issued by the Union Government on February 19,1991, under Environment Protection Act, 1986.[161]

Villages along the sea coast and natural saline canals were under threat due to conversion of land into acquaculture farms and the traditional fishermen had lost their landing ground facilities for fish catch, the report noted.[162]

The Supreme Court on November 30, 1995 in what is know as "Delhi hazardous industries-pollution matter" directed the commissioner, Delhi Municipal Corporation (MCD) not to issue any licenses hence forth for 'hazardous' or 'obnoxious' industries in the 'residential' or non-conforming areas' within its (MCD's) jurisdiction.[162A]

The Bench also ordered the Commissioner, not to henceforth register such industries within the jurisdiction of MCD.[162B]

The Bench consisting of Mr. Justice Kuldip Singh and Mr. Justice Saghir Ahmad made these orders when a public interest litigation writ petition from Mr. M.C. Mehta, an advocate, *inter alia* seeking shifting of such hazardous or obnoxious industries from 'residential' or 'non-conforming areas' in Delhi came up for futher hearing.[162C]

The court expressed surprise when it was told that the MCD was issuing new industrial licences and renewing the old ones even as the Court was taking steps for allocation of such hazardous industries from residential or non-conforming areas in Delhi.[162D]

The Bench while observing that any violation of its direction would attract 'contempt of court', directed the Commissioner, to file within two weeks indicating the number of such industries.[162E]

The Supreme Court on December 7, 1995 imposed a fine of Rs. 10,000 on 150 industries in the capital for their failure to instal anti-pollution devices as directed earlier by the Court.[162F]

The fine was directed to be paid within two weeks and all the polluting industries were asked to instal the device within six weeks. Failure on any of these two counts would lead to the closure of the industry, the court said.[162G]

The fine was imposed by a Division Bench comprising Mr. Justice Kuldip Singh and Mr. Justice Shaghir Ahmad during the continued hearing on a public interest petition.[162H]

The above discussions give an idea that the Indian judiciary right from the later part of the 19th century till todate has been actively contributing to the cause of environmental protection. It has always maintained a balance in cases of conflicts in between environmental protection and development. The judiciary has been very cautious with regard to PIL cases. It has never been prejudiced and has acted to the cause of socio-economic justice. Whenever there has been revengeful attitude in the filing of PIL cases, the same has been rightly discouraged by the courts specially the Apex Court.

REFERENCES

1. *Supra* note 2 of Chapter II.
2. *Khair Din and others* v. *Wasan Singh and others*, AIR, 1935 Lahore 28; *Bheera* v. *Tara Singh*, 1927 All 267-99 IC 415-25 Cr. L.J. 159-49 All. 270; *Emperor* v. *Fazal Din* (1911) 91C 891-12 Cr. L.J. 146; *Shadi* v. *Empress* (1888) 17 PR 1888 Cr.; *Emperor* v. *Sita Ram* (1917) 32 PR 1917-41 IC 1000-18 Cr L.J. 888; *Achhru* v. *Emperor*, 1930 Lah 662-125 IC 613-31 Cr L J 880-11 Lah 247; *Srinath* v. *Ainaddi Halder*, (1897) 24 Cal 395-IC W N 217; *Churahu Das* v. *Shakaraj Das*, 1926 All 157-91 I C 59-27 Cr L J 27; *Baisakhi Ram* v. *Emperor*, 1930 Lah 361-1930 Cr C 965-120 IC 796-31 Cr L J 167.
3. *Emperor* v. *Nama Ram* 6 Bom L.R. 52 (1904).
4. 7 MP LR 103 (1910).
5. *Atma Singh* v. *State of Punjab and others*, CLR 1973–77 Supp.; *Ratan Singh* v. *Mohinder Singh*, 1973 CLR 278; *Gain Singh and others* v. *State of Punjab and others*, 1979 CLR 278; See also *Mool Chand* v. *State of Hydrabad and another* 1973–77 Supp. 403.
6. AIR 1979 SC 143 decided by Y.V. Chandrachud C.J., R.S. Sarkaria and O. Chinappa Reddy JJ on 15.9.1978.
7. AIR 1980 SC 1622 at page 1638 (Judgement was delivered by Krishna Iyer and O. Chinappa Reddy JJ).
8. *Ibid* para 1 at page 1622.
9. *Ibid.*
10. *Tarsem Singh and others* v. *Mukand Singh Mistry and others*, 1981 SCC 223 decided on 12.5.1981.
11. *Ramlal* v. *Bari Singh and another*, 1982 GCC 189 decided on 26.2 1982.
12. *Supra* note 7.
13. *Supra* note 6.
14. SCC 1979 All L. J. 456; 1976 Cut. L. R. 127; 1973 BLTR 79; AIR, 1958 Pat. 210; AIR 1939 (Lah. 279 and 452); 1974 Cr. L.J. 1230; 1970 All WR 828; (1964) Cr. L.J. 94 (MP); 1962 2 Cr. L.J. 413 All.; AIR 1943 Pat. 32; 1939 Pat. 383; 1927 Pat. 265; 1954 Cal. 560; 7 Beng L.R. 499 (1833) 2 Weiv. 58.
15. The Act received the assent of the President on March 29, 1985 and was published in the Gazette of India on the same date. The Act replaced an Ordinance which the President had promulgated on February 20, 1985 for the same purpose.
16. The plaint does not allege precise damages suffered by the persons having claims. The amended plaint estimates the value of total claims to exceed Rs. 3,9000 crores "if the case is tried to judgement through all the stages."
17. In November, 1986, two non-governmental organisations representing some victims, applied to the District Court for "immediate relief". Thereafter, on April

2, 1987 Judge Deo placed his proposal to grant "reconciliatory substantial interim relief" before the parties. This proposal culminated in Judge Deo's December 18,1987 order awarding interim compensatation.

17A. *S.C. issues notice to Union Carbide*, The Hindu, dated 2.12.1995, p. 13.
17B. *Ibid.*
17C. *Ibid.*
17D. *Ibid.*
17E. *Ibid.*
17F. *Ibid.*
17G. *Ibid.*
18. (1986)2 SCC 176 and AIR 1987 SC 965 (1st case).
19. Pande J.N., Constitutional Law of India, 1991, p. 227.
20. *Supra* note 18.
21. *Special Environment Court soon, The Hindu,* Visakhapatnam, dated 26.6.92,p.4.
22. *Bill of environment tribunal moved, The Hindu,* Visakhapatnam, dated 25.5.95, p. 15.
23. *Ibid.*
24. *Ibid.*
25. *Ibid.*
26. *Ibid.*
27. *M.C. Mehta* v. *Union of India* (1987) 4 SCC 463 (2nd case). The final judgement in this case was given on 12.1.1988.
28. Jariwala C.M., *Direction of Environmental Justice in India: Critical Appraisal of 1987 Case Law*, 35 JILI, 1993, p. 94.
29. *Ibid.*
30. *M.C. Mehta* v. *Union of India*, AIR 1987 SC 1086 (3rd case).
31. Justice Madon was to retire on 6.4.1987 and hence did not find a place in the larger bench.
32. *Supra* note 28 p. 100.
33. *Supra* note 30 at p. 1089.
34. *Ibid* at p. 1091 quoted *supra* note 32.
35. *Supra* note 28 at p. 101.
36. *Ibid.*
37. (1968) 19 LT 220 quoted *ibid.*
38. *Supra* note 18.
39. *Supra* note 33.
40. *Ibid.*
41. UJ (SC) 1987 (2), 595.
42. UJ (SC) 1987(1) 265.
43. AIR 1987 Kant. 82.
44. AIR., 1987 SC 1190.
45. XXIII ASIL (1987), p. 102.
46. *Kisan Sahakari Chini Mills* v. *State*, A.I.R. 1987 All. 298.
47. The object and reason of the Cess Act stated that the cess was imposed "to financially help the Water Boards" for the prevention and control of water pollution.
48. *Supra* note 28 p. 104–5.
49. *Ibid.*
50. AIR., 1987 SC 374.
51. *Ibid.*

52. *Supra* note 28 p. 106.
53. AIR., 1987 SC 359. See earlier decision of the Supreme Court in this, Air 1985 SC 652, where the Supreme Court tilted the balance in favour of the environment. The court in the instant case realised that its order "would undoubtedly cause hardship" but it opined, "it is a price that has to be paid". *Id.* at 656.
54. *Supra* note 52 id.
55. *Supra* note 45 p. 98.
56. *Ibid*, p. 99.
57. AIR., 1987 SC 1073.
58. *Supra* note 28 p. 107.
59. *State of Bihar* v. *Banshi Ram Modi*, AIR, 1985 SC 814.
60. *Supra* note 58 p. 107.
61. *Supra* note 57.
62. *Supra* note 60 id.
63. *Ibid* p.108.
64. *Ibid.*
65. *Calcutta Youth Front* v. *State of WB*, UJ (SC) 1987 (2) 576; *Sachidananda Pandey* c. *State of WB*, AIR 1987, SC 1109; *Damodar Rao* v. *S.O. Municipality Corpn.* Hyd. AIR, 1987 AP 171.
66. AIR., 1988 Raj. 2.
67. *Ibid* at p. 4.
68. XXIV ASIL (1988), p. 135.
69. Quoted *ibid*, AIR, 1988 Raj. 4.
70. (1988)2 SCC 115.
71. *Supra* note 68.
72. *Ibid.*
73. *Ibid.*
74. *Rural Litigation & Entitlement Kendra* v. *State of U.P.*, AIR 1988 SC 2187.
75. AIR AIR 1989 SC 594.
76. XXV ASIL (1989) p. 58.
77. (1990) Supp. SCC 151.
78. XXVI ASIL (1990) p. 185.
79. *Ibid.*
80. *Ibid.*
81. AIR 1990 Ker 321.
82. *Supra* note 80.
83. *Ibid.*
84. XXVII ASIL (1991), p. 41–42.
85. (1991) 4 SCC 137.
86. XXVII ASIL (1991; p. 42).
87. *Supra* note 85.
88. *Ibid.*
89. (1991) 2 SCC 353.
90. *Supra* note 86.
91. *Ibid.*
92. *Ibid.*
93. *Ibid.*
94. (1991) 1 SCC 598.
95. *Supra* note 90, p. 43.
96. *Supra* note 94 at p. 604.

97. *Ibid.*
98. (1991) 4 SCC 54.
99. *Supra* note 90, p. 44.
100. *Supra* note 98 at p. 74 (The Bench comprised T.K. Thommen and R.M. Sahi JJ).
101. (1991) 2 SCC 539.
102. *Ibid* at p. 541.
103. *R.L. & E Kendra, Dehradun* v. *State of U.P.*, AIR 1985 SC 652.
104. *R.L. & E Kendra, Dehradun* v. *State of U.P.*, (1989) Supp. 1 SCC 504.
105. *Supra* note 99, p. 45.
106. (1991) 3 SCC 347.
107. *Supra* note 105 *ibid.*
108. *Ibid.*
109. *Ibid.*
110. *Ibid.*
111. A.I.R. 1982 SC 382.
112. XXVIII ASIL (1992) p. 240.
113. *Ibid.*
114. AIR 1992 Kant 57.
115. *Inid* at 66–67.
116. *Supra* note 112 at p. 241.
117. *Supra* note 116 p. 241.
118. *Supra* note 114 at 65.
119. *Supra* note 117 *id.*
120. AIR 1992 Kant 256.
121. *Supra* note 117 *id.*
122. *Supra* note 74.
123. *State of Himachal Pradesh* v. *Parent of a Student of Medioal College, Simla* AIR 1985 SC 910.
124. *Supra* note 121 p. 242.
125. AIR, 1992 Bom 471.
126. *Supra* note 126 *id.*
126A. *Ibid.*
127. AIR, 1992 Ori 225
128. *Supra* note 121 at 242.
129. *Ibid.*
130. *Ibid.*
131. *Ibid.*
132. *Ibid.*
133. AIR, 1193 H.P. 52.
134. *Ibid.* at 53.
135. *Ibid.*
136. AIR, 1993 Cal. 215.
137. *Ibid.* 216.
138. AIR, 1993 A.P. 257.
139. AIR, 1985 SC 910.
140. *Supra* note 138 at p. 272.
141. AIR, 1991 SC 420.
142. AIR, 1993 Ker 297.
143. *Ibid.*
144. AIR, 1993 Ker 320.

145. *Ibid.*
146. AIR, 1994 Ori 191.
147. AIR, 1995 Ori 84.
148. *Ibid* at p. 88.
149. Bar on industries in coastal zone confirmed, The Hindu, Visakhapatnam dated March 10, 1995.
150. *Ibid.*
151. *Ibid.*
152. *Ibid.*
153. *Ibid.*
154. *Ibid.*
154A. *Sc Orders closure of 59 t.N. Tanneries,* The Hindu Visakhapatnam May 2, 1995 at p. 1
154B. *Ibid.*
154C. *Ibid.*
154D. *Ibid.*
154E. *Ibid.*
154F. *Ibid.*
154G. *Ibid.*
155. *Ban on farm land use for acquaculture*, Aqua International, July, 1995 p. 30.
156. *Ibid.*
157. *Ibid.*
158. *Ibid.*
159. *Ibid.*
160. *Ibid.*
161. *Ibid.*
162. *Ibid.*
162A. *SC directive to Delhi Corporation*, The Hindu, Visakhapatnam, dt. 1.12.95, p. 13.
162B. *Ibid*
162C. *Ibid.*
162D. *Ibid.*
162E. *Ibid.*
162F. *150 industries fined for pollution*, The Hindu, Visakhapatnam, dated 7.12.1955 p.1.
162G. *Ibid.*
162H. *Ibid.*

CHAPTER VI

ENVIRONMENTAL EDUCATION

Global Perspective

The concept of Environmental Education (EE) has been undergoing changes ever since the world at large started waking up to the significance of the role played by the environment in human life and vice versa. Not that the importance of the environment *per se* had ever been doubted by humanity as the deification of diverse elements of nature in practicality and the ancient religions also testify the same belief. But for a long time the environment—mostly understood as Nature—continued to be perceived as part of the heavenly order, something immutable and permanent, with which humanity could have no more than a totally submissive relationship.[1]

The earth's environment has changed more rapidly in the past generation than at any other comparable time in history, one of the primary sources of these dynamics being precipitated by human interaction with the biosphere.[2]

Agriculture, forestry, energy production, human population increase with its socio-economic repercussions, have been considered to a great extent, responsible for alterations in the earth's eco-system resulting in global warming, ozone depletion, loss of biodiversity, which are but a few of the alterations that transcend national boundaries and must be viewed on a global perspective.[3]

Although some controversy is possible regarding the entire spectrum of environmental issues involved in global change, there could be a broad agreement on the key ones. The following diagram gives an idea of the majority of the key and subordinate issues involved in global

Global Change and Key Issues

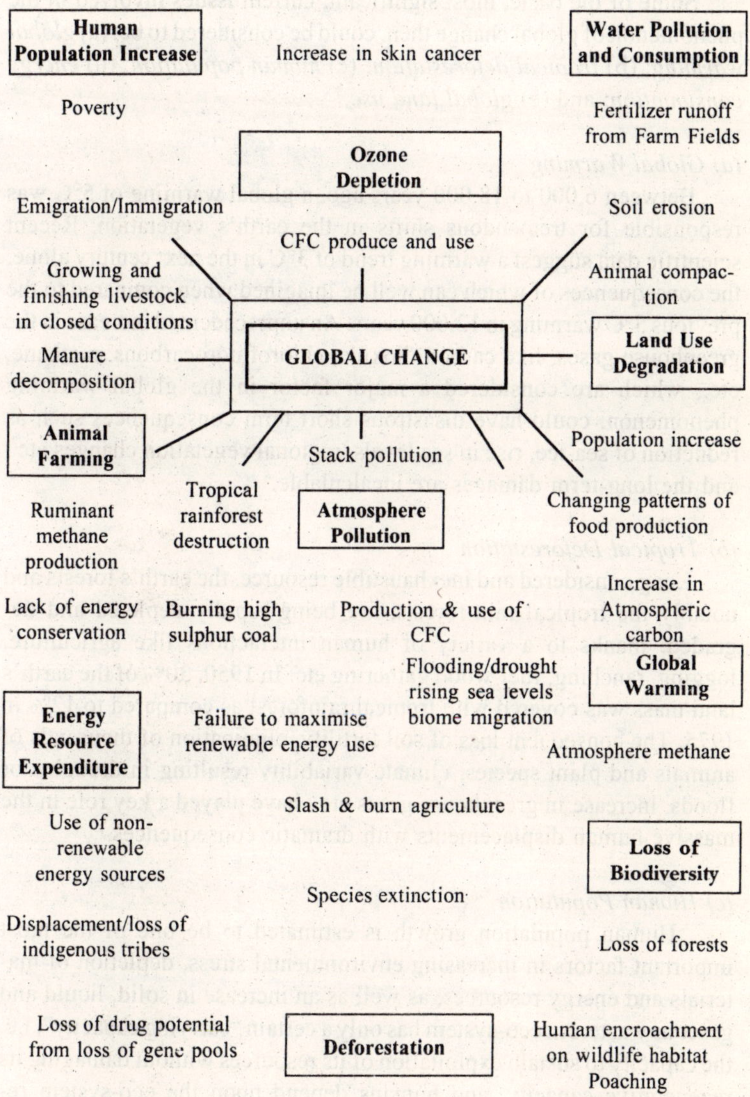

change, without trying to precise all the interactions among them which are far too numerous and complex.[4]

Some of the basic, most significant, current issues involved in the phenomenon of global change then, could be considered to be: (a) *global warming*; (b) *tropical deforestation*; (c) *human population*; (d) *energy consumption*; and (e) *global land use*.[5]

(a) Global Warming

Between 6,000 to 18,000 years ago, a global warming of 5°C was responsible for tremendous shifts in the earth's vegetation. Recent scientific data suggest a warming trend of 3°C in the next century alone, the consequences of which can well be imagined when compared to the previous 5°C warming in 12,000 years. An unprecedented increase in the greenhouse gases, like carbon dioxide, chlorofluorocarbons, methane, etc., which are considered a major factor in the global warming phenomenon, could have disastrous short term consequences such as reduction of sea-ice, rise in sea levels, regional vegetation changes etc., and the long-term damages are incalculable.[6]

(b) Tropical Deforestation

Long considered and inexhaustible resource, the earth's forests and notably the tropical rain-forests, are being rapidly depleted and degraded, thanks to a variety of human interactions like agriculture, logging, ranching, fuel-wood gathering etc. In 1950, 30% of the earth's land mass was covered with tropical rainforest as compared to 12% in 1975. The consequent loss of soil fertility, elimination of thousands of animals and plant species, climate variability resulting in droughts or floods, increase in greenhouse gases etc., have played a key role in the massive human displacements with dramatic consequences.[7]

(c) Human Population

Human population growth is estimated to be one of the most important factors in increasing environmental stress, depletion of materials and energy resources, as well as an increase in solid, liquid and gaseous waste. An eco-system has only a certain "carrying capacity", i.e. the capacity to sustain exploitation of its resources without damaging its regenerative capacity, and humans depend upon the eco-system resources for survival, it is vital to harmonize human population growth with the environmental reality i.e. the carrying capacity of the concerned eco-system.[8]

(d) Energy Consumption

Since 1900, world consumption of fossil fuels has increased nearly 4 times as fast as world population. Major sources of fossil fuel—petrol, natural gas and coal, are expected to last for respectively for 35–50, 60–80 and about 200 years. However, it is not only the depletion of these non-renewable energy sources that is cause for concern, but equally, the generation of harmful by-products due to their excessive utilization like smog, acid precipitation, petrol spills, or global warming.[9]

(e) Global Land Use

Of the 13 billion hectares of land on earth, 31% is forested, 25% is rangeland and 11% is cultivated—33% being classified as "wasteland". As the first three categories supply a large portion of the resources utilized by humans and since the beginning of humanity, control and use of this land has been an essential aspect of human survival, the rapid growth of both human population and consumption has not only increased the variety of its uses but also the severity of the impact of the usage resulting in what is termed as land degradation and due to which the actual amount of land which can be utilised, is shrinking. In 1948 it was estimated that 35% of the earth's land surface was in peril and that approximately 6 million hectares of land were being destroyed annually, the primary causes of land degradation being overgrazing, overcultivation, salinization and deforestation leading to soil erosion, floods, loss of vegetation, droughts, desertification, poverty.[10]

All these global change issues, in order to be dealt effectively, require concerted efforts on the part of all nations since the phenomenon of global change is not limited by any sort of frontiers. Unfortunately for a variety of economic, political, religions or other reasons, it is at present difficult to arrive at sustained and harmonious world-wide action in this respect. However, if these issues are approached in a manner so as to produce educational outcomes related to changing human behaviour then, in the coming years, the direction of these behaviour changes could lead to a resolution—partly, if not wholly—of the issues.[11]

In other words, adopting the right strategies to involve people in the search for solutions and providing them with the knowledge, the skills and the motivations is absolutely vital in dealing with the pehnomenon of global change. This could be achieved through *environmental education* whose objective is to develop a world population that is aware of, and concerned about, *environment and development and associated problems*, and which has the *knowledge, skills*, attitude, motivations and commitment to work individually and collectively toward solutions of current problems and the prevention of new ones.[12]

Forming *environmentally responsible citizens* being its avowed goal, environmental education is a major vehicle for imparting global change instruction since, as stated earlier, the resolution—partly, if not wholly—of global change issues depends largely upon behaviour change in humans brought about by proper education.[13]

Of course, it is necessary not to lose sight of the fact that translating these objectives into instructional reality represent no mean task for the education system since, although traditional thinking would have us believe that knowledge leads to awarness which results in action, research findings seem to show that the process leading to responsible behaviour is not quite so direct or straight forward and that there are quite a few variables to be taken into account like cognizance of the courses of most effective action available, skill is applying knowledge to the concerned issues, an act, not to mention situational factors such as economic constraints, social pressure, opportunities to choose different courses of action etc.[14]

Besides, in the specific case of global change instruction through environmental education, educationalists are faced with an additional challenge; making learners capable of viewing global change holistically and at the same time being able to analyse individual issues at local regional levels. There are also a certain number of problems that arise due to (a) lack of sufficient data in certain areas; (b) doubts regarding the accuracy and significance of existing date; and (c) the variety of interpretations of certain phenomena due to differing political, economic, religious and social values.[15]

At the school level, two major approaches, among others, are recommendable with regard to global change instruction: *Extended Case Study and Issues Investigation and Action.*[16]

The *Extended Case Study* approach consists largely of a teacher-directed analysis of a particular issue, using both primary and secondary sources to deliver issue-focused information and skills to learners. On being oriented to the issue, the teachers enable the students to investigate the issue on a group level. Once a group decision with respect to the issue is reached, remediation can be embarked upon. This method provides flexibility and control by the teacher but also involves a lot of time, energy and skill in putting together a case study.[17]

In contrast, in *Issue Investigation and Action*, a broader and more generalised approach is employed—the intention being to develop skills in issue investigation and resolution which can be applied throughout one's life. This method provides for definition, practice and application of knowledge and skills for independent investigation and resolution of issues so as to develop autonomous investigations.[18]

A *goal-oriented framework* could also be used as a basis for organizing instructional strategies. For example making use of simulations, models, reading etc., to lay the ecological foundations; *case-histories*, field trips, brainstorming sessions, discussions etc., for creating *conceptual awareness*; secondary source investigations, primary data collection, value clarification, moral education . . . for *investigation skill* and evaluation of issues; and action workshops, action learning in community interaction, action analysis projects for *environment action skills*.[19]

Given the vital importance of imparting global change instruction in schools and the interdiscplinary nature of the subject, the most effective way to do so would be to incorporate it into the existing curricula. However, while doing so it is essential to keep in mind certain broad principles so that the curriculum provides for:[20]

1. An in-depth knowledge of issues;
2. Teaching skills of issue analysis and investigation;
3. Teaching citizenship skills for issue remediation;
4. An attempt to develop an internal locus of control.

In the specific setting of secondary school education, global change instruction could be "infused" into the existing curriculum by integrating global change contents and skills into existing courses so as to focus on these contents/ skills without jeopardising the courses themselves. Courses in agriculture, home economics, health, science, social studies or language arts could lend themselves perfectly well to this sort of infusion. A key component of the infusion process however, is co-operation from the staff members responsible for the infused programmes as its effectiveness depends largely on the their willingness to build together an infusion plan and see it carried out.[21]

Environmental Education for Pre-schoolers

Environmental education for pre-schoolers is based on the concept that fostering a sense of wonder and appreciation for the world is important to the development of young children and the preservation of Planet Earth and consists of a curriculum guide, resource library and network.[22]

The curriculum guide is entitled *Fostering a Sense of Wonder during the Early Childhood* and is meant for early childhood educators. It offers suggestions on how to foster in young children a sense of appreciation and caring for the natural world; ideas on using "pro-nature" books with children; suggestions for indoor discovery activities and outdoor excursion as well as annotated bibliography of related resources.[23]

The resource library contains over 100 different items relating to environmental education for pre-schoolers on nature-related topics such as gardening, animals in the classroom, earth art activities, nature in the city etc. In addition to printed materials, video and audio tapes are also available.[24]

The network is committed to the development, expansion and evaluation of quality programmes in early childhood education. It sponsors information-sharing meetings and written communications.[25]

Environmental Education in the Commonwealth

The International Conference on Environmental Education (EE) in the Commonwealth was held at the University of Bradford, U.K., from 18–23 July 1993. Supported by various national and international organisations including UNESCO, UNEP, CIDA, SIDA, CTZ, the Commonwealth Secretariat, the UK Department of Education, etc., it brought together over 80 delegates from around 40 Commonwealth countries representing UN organisations and agencies, GOs, NGOs. academic institutions and bilateral agencies.

The conference was aimed at catalysing and promoting the systematic development of environmental education programmes in Commonwealth countries. Its major objectives being:[27]

- to enable exchange of experience amongst governmental and non-governmental EE specialists and practitioners in Commonwealth countries;
- to stimulate contacts amongst those working with EE for the establishment of working links and networks;
- to discuss long-term strategies for the development of EE in the Commonwealth.

In the Declaration approved by the plenary session of the conference, the following recommendations were addressed to the Commonwealth Heads of Government:[28]

- It is necessary to formally acknowledge the importance of EE in the process of finding the way for sustainable development for all;
- It is necessary to develop national policies for EE, thus meeting the target set in Chapter 36 of Agenda 21 (Education, Awarness and Training).
- It is necessary to ensure that EE is included at all levels of the formal and non-formal education process and to support existing mechanisms to implement EE programme addressing the training and resource needs seen in Commonwealth countries.
- It is necessary to Disseminate EE in the framework of existing Commonwealth structures and to promote cooperation among them, nationally and internationally, maximising the use of resources and funds.

It was also strongly recommended that the Declaration be brought to the attention of the next Commonwealth Ministers of Education meeting in 1994 to ensure that this important topic is included in the agenda of the next Commonwealth Heads of Government meeting in 1995.[29]

National Perspective

Environmentalists all over the country must be grateful to the Supreme Court for having directed the Union and State governments and the University Grants Commission to create environmental awarness among the students and the public.[30] Although the fourth estate has contributed a great deal in highlighting some of the crucial problems of environment, the government on its part has not done enough.[31]

Mere conditional clearances by expert committee and pollution control boards cannot ensure safety of the environment. Only environmental awarness among the people can make them put up a united fight to protect their own health and environment.[32]

Unfortunately, most of the ministers and bureaucrats in the Ministries of Environment, Health, Education, Tourism Industry, Information and Broadcasting and Social Welfare do not seem to be genuinely interested in protecting the environment as envisaged under Article 49 of the Constitution.[33]

Nor are the Ministries making any sincere efforts despite the devastating effects of pollution in the industrial belts of Bombay, Delhi, Calcutta, Agra, Madras, Cochin, Hyderabad, Visakhapatnam, Durgapur, Talcher, Baroda, Ramagundam, Kothagudem Yerraguntla and Thane.[33]

It is reported that the people of Bombay are spending Rs. 500 crores per year towards medical expenses for the sickness caused by air pollution from automobiles and industries. Nearly 80 per cent of the natural water course is seriously polluted by liquid wastes from municipalities and industries.[34]

All such hazards can be attributed to the lack of minimum degree of environmental awarness among the educated elite and the common masses. Even the devastating impact of Bhopal gas tragedy and the Delhi gas leak accident have not opened the eyes of the government and the universities to incorporate ecological and environmental considerations in planning and development activities and recast the teaching and research programmes at the school, college and university levels.[35]

In order to conserve the natural environmental quality and develop human resources that constitute the basic foundation for meaningful economic growth, people must be educated on crucial topics like pollution, pollution management, forestry, wildlife, health and natural resources, conservation through print and electronic media and revised educational curricula. It is hoped that the UGC and the Central and State governments will now atleast move in the right direction to ensure the survival of plant, animal and human populations so that there is no conflict between environment and development.[36]

Learning the Green Letter of the Law[37]

At an open public trial, the Adivasi Kalyankari Sangh, a tribal society based in Bastar (MP), moves the court. The MP Tendu Pata Act, 1964 has usurped the customary rights of the tribals to collect tendu leaves in which *beedis* are rolled. The State, instead, has monopolised the tendu trade with the aid of an unjust law. The flourishing *beedi* industry now fetches the government Rs. 65 crores per year. But the tribals, the original owners of the forest and now turned labourers, remain paupers earning a paltry fee.

The above scene, however, is fictitious—a kind of a theatre, recently put up by the year-old Centre for Environmental Law at WWF, at its first convocation ceremony at which a batch of 30 students received their diploma certificates on completion of a course in Environmental Law.

Says Prof. Chatrapati Singh, founder of the centre, which has been set up with government and international assistance including the Ford Foundation "Our environment laws are in a mess and neither do they have a place in the curriculum, while the teaching of law does not provide practical understanding of cases. The purpose behind the fictitious court trial was to give our future lawyers some practical training as they actually went to MP to collect all relevant data."

A premier institute of its kind in the country and South Asia, the Centre for Environmental Law (CEL) was set up to improve the study of environment laws, build up public and legal awareness and develop human resources for the effective use of the legal system in environmental issues.

Prof. Singh points out that environmental laws deals with the distribution of natural resources of the country—land, water, forest, mineral and metals—the wealth of a nation. Unless people's right to natural resources are protected, they will always remain poor. Sound laws can alone ensure equitable distribution of resources, an imbalance of which is the basic cause of poverty.

India, today, has a plethora of environmental law. And notwithstanding the national environment policy, a tilt exists in favour of political, industrial and urban bosses. But under Article 13 of the Indian Constitution,[38] all laws that violate the fundamental rights of the people can be reviewed and repealed. One of the major aims of the CEL, hence, is to be instrumental changing the legal system making it serve disadvantaged people through legal education and reform.[39]

Environmentalists note that our environmental laws are difficult to implement because they contain contradictions. For example, the ministry of environment has one policy, while the ministry of industry has another. No serious attention had been paid to the rational behind environmental legislation which blindly follow inherited colonial tradition. Hence, the State has overriding power over natural resources.[40]

Says Prof. Singh: "Tribals form seven per cent of our population—as large as that of Australia. But the right of the tribals are totally neglected as are the rights of 85 per cent of rural people. The state forest laws, e.g., grant the government the right to cut down trees and sell timber to industries at a discount. But the use of fuel-wood and forest produce for survival by the local people is considered as theft. Worse still are laws dealing with water."[41]

There are also several technical hitches that make environmental laws difficult to implement and litigation a time-consuming, inconclusive affair. Besides offences under the environment laws are lumped under the Indian Penal Code. The stigma of criminal charges against officials and executives often result in avoidance of persecution. The penalties made are extremely soft compared to the big damages.[42]

The CEL hopes to tackle the whole body of environmental laws in the long run and also eventually define the international agenda in environmental issues by safeguarding the interest of developing countries of South Asia which markedly differ from that of developed nations. Presently, it has started its battle on home grounds, co-ordinating litigations and making lawyers, judges and legislators green minded. "We hope to shortly move the Supreme Court on behalf of the tribals of Bastar. If we can establish their right to tendu leaves, we will establish their right to life," says Prof. Singh.[43]

Until quite recently the function of law was viewed to be a function of social control, i.e., trying to regulate human behaviour in general. The social complexities arising out to technological revolution and the problems of telescoping a vast and all-involving transformation of traditional social structure in developing countries have made law an instrument of social change also. The function of law, therefore, is not only to preserve existing social value and interpret them so as to adjust them suitably to slow and gradual change but to create new values and also see to it that the new values are implemented at a quicker space.[44] Friedmann had rightly pointed out that it would be tragic if the laws are unable to respond to the changing conditions.[45] The developing societies, in particular, are going through a transformation through legislative enactments. India is also bringing about socio-economic changes through the instrument of law. If the law schools are to play an important role in modern India, they have to orient themselves in such a way that legal education satisfies the changing socio-politico-economic needs of the society. Today, in consequence of rapid industrialization and urbanization, the environmental pollution is spreading fast and poses serious danger to the survival of the living species throughout the world. On the other hand the ignorance of pollution hazards has made the human survival a difficult one. This can be minimised by educating the society in protecting and controlling environmental pollution. The Law Schools can play an important role by imparting education in Environmental Jurisprudence.

Global change, though a dramatic and potent reality for human beings, is still an extremely difficult phenomenon to conceptualize mainly because of the complexity of the dynamics and the number of issues involved. However, if educators, keeping in mind the holistic nature of the problem as well as the interrelations of the individual issues that go to form it, set their sights on the attainment of the goals of environmental education i.e. awareness, attitudes, skills, motivation, commitment and ethical responsibility, they will be well on the path to the formation of environmentally responsible citizens of tomorrow. For it is they, who will be able to outweigh the factors—whether political, economic, social or cultural—that at present prevent the implementation of effective actions to counteract the negative effects of the phenomenon of global change as well as prevent the recurrence of problems that have arisen in the past.[46]

In view of the above discussion the following are suggested:

Curriculum:

- National goals for EE teaching should be clearly stated;
- An EE curriculum should be developed and integrated into present subjects.
- Specific objectives should be formulated with regard to acquiring knowledge, awarness, and developing investigative, action and evaluation skills.
- Research programmes on environmental issues and education should be established.
- Environmental Education should be made compulsory both at the LL.B. and LL.M. levels.

Teacher Training :

- EE in-service teachers training should be provided based on an assessment of the needs.
- A set of basic EE competencies should be formulated for all secondary school teachers.

Non-formal Education :

- Organisations should cooperate to make use of existing non-formal education programmes and infra-structure before developing new initiatives.
- Training in non-formal EE should be provided to both trainers and trainees.
- A national policy on non-formal EE should be formulated, supported by adequate legislation.

Actions :

- EE workshops should be provided for academic staff.
- Competitions, prizes, entertainment should be organised to reward positive student actions.

- Funds should be sought for EE programmes and support system for their implementation.

Conclusion

Earlier it has been discussed that environmental problems may relate to the degradation of biosphere resources or of the quality of habitat conditions, that these problems may be of limited local dimension, may extend to a larger regional scale, or may be world-wide. One factor that seems prominent relates to escalating population numbers and consumption. Problems of poverty, including hunger, mal-nutrition and recurrent famine, are rampant in under-developed countries, where the population increases at rates that are much higher than those of economic development. Income disparities are flagrant, social and political strife are common features, and indigenous capabilities for managing development and environmental issues are weak.

It has also been discussed that world community has yet to develop effective capabilities for managing global environmental issues. Some of these issues threaten the survival of all. Technological means may be available, but political will seems short. In an article entitled "The Environment of Tomorrow," Holdgate (1991) sets the time horizon of tomorrow at the year 2030. He enumerates six principal environmental trends that are ". . . likely to prove unstoppable on a 40-year scale; a dramatic increase in the world population, deforestation, land degradation, including desertification, loss of biological diversity, population and climate change." He notes that solution to these problems ". . . does not lie in science and technology, but in politics." The word "unstoppable"means that the problems cannot be stopped in the socio-political set up now prevailing.

During the 80s, the world scientific community became better informed about environment and development issues, and came to realise that technological fixes need to to be supported by sociological transformation. Comparing the World Conservation Strategy (IUNC, 1990) and Caring for the Earth (IUCN, 1991) produced by the same partnership (IUCN-UNEP-WWF), it is found that the evolution of environmental thinking during the decade. The former document advocates a type of development that conserve the vitality and diversity of the biosphere, the latter confirms this requisite and adds to it the necessity of improving the quality of human life and the active participation of people in development planning and implementation.

Several provisions of the Acts are also being misused or misinterpreted, which defeat the very objective of the laws. The Environment Protection Act, for instance, allows for community action against companies responsible for polluting the environment. A 60-day notice is required to be given to the State pollution board before filing a suit against the industrial unit. This provision is often misused. A notice may never be given if the people do not know the law, and they would thus not be able to go to court. But even if a notice is given, the boards simply ignores it.

The evidence required to convict a pollution industry in terms of air and water samples has to be collected by the board authorities. This means that an unwilling board can stall the proceedings by not taking samples at all.

Likewise, the Factories Act stipulates that submitting a detailed disaster management plan is mandatory for hazardous units, which must be produced on demand by any member of the public. Yet, this never happens. Even public sector companies flout this provision and the law remains only on paper. No individual can ever obtain the disaster management plan, which in many cases is not available. For many units, the Official Secrets Act is invoked and the stock reply is given that it is not in the public interest to know these things. Nuclear plants and power projects have traditionally done this kind of stonewalling.

It is perhaps because of this that public interest litigation has entered the area of environmental protection. Several successful cases have resulted from this. It has proved to be of immense benefit to the society so far as environmental protection cases are concerned. It has worked like an oasis in the desert of despotism.

The judical attitude is found to have been changed from time to time. The judiciary, specially from 1980 onwards has played a constructive role. It has maintained a balance between environmental protection and development. In all the M.C. Mehta cases, what deserves appreciation, is the social service rendered by M.C. Mehta, a Senior Advocate of the Supreme Court of India. He, as has been rightly pointed out by the court, "though lone and single," "has fought a valiant battle against a giant enterprise and achieved substantial success." In the present world, having more of a commercialised rather than socialised approach, social service lawyers are like an oasis in the desert. What is needed in the administration of environmental justice today, is the presence of such dedicated lawyers and social workers, who can withstand powerful pressure of the capitalists and save India's environment from further degradation.[47]

Last but not the least is the suggestion given for environmental education. If this could be followed, then the society can be saved from further deterioration.

REFERENCES

1. *Connect*, UNESCO-UNEP Environmental Education Newsletter, Vol. XX No. 2, June 1995.
2. *Ibid.* Vol. XVIII, No.1, March 1993.
3. *Ibid.*
4. *Ibid.*
5. *Futuresco*, A UNESCO bibliographical bulletin of futre-oriented Literature, Environment, Nos. 2-3, July 1992, June 1993.
6. *Ibid.*
7. *Ibid.*
8. *Ibid.*
9. *Ibid.*
10. *Ibid.*
11. *Surpa* note 2.
12. *Ibid.*
13. *Ibid.*
14. *Ibid.*
15. *Ibid.*
16. *Ibid.*
17. *Ibid.*
18. *Ibid.*
19. *Ibid.*
20. *Ibid.*
21. *Ibid.*
22. *Connect*, UNESCO-UNEP Environmental Education Newsletter, Vol. XVIII, No. 2, June 1993.
23. *Ibid.*
24. *Ibid.*
25. For detail information, write to Dr. Ruth Wilson, Project Director, 418 Education Building, Bowling Green State University, Bowling Green, OH 43403, USA.
26. *Connect*, UNESCO-UNEP Environmental Education Newsletter, Vol. XVIII No. 3 September, 1993.
27. *Ibid.*
28. *Ibid.*
29. For Proceedings of the conference contact: University of Bradford, Research Unit on EE and Development, Bradford BD7 IDP.
30. *M.C. Mehta* v. *Union of India*, AIR 1992 SC 382.
31. Rao, T. Shivaji, *Environmental Education*, The Hindu, Vishakhapatnam dated March 3, 1993.
32. *Ibid.*

33. It shall be the obligation to the State of protect every monument or place or object of artistic or historic interest, declared by or under law made by Parliament to be of national importance, from spoilation, disfigurment, destruction, removal, disposal or export, as the case may be.
34. *Surpa* note 31.
35. *Ibid.*
36. *Ibid.*
37. The Sunday Time of India, New Delhi, March 20, 1994 p. 22.
38. *Article 13: Laws inconsistent with or in derogation of the fundamental rights:*
 (1) All laws in force in the territory of India immediately before the commencement of this Constitution, if so far as they are inconsistent with the provisions of this part, shall, to the extent of such inconsistency, be void.
 (2) The State shall not make any law which takes away or abridges the rights conferred by this Part and any law made in contravention of this clause shall, to the extent to the contravention, be void.
 (3) In this article, unless the context otherwise requires.-
  (a) "law" includes any Ordinance, order, bye-law, rule regulation, notification, custom or usage having in the territory of India the force of law;
  (b) "law in force" includes laws passed or made by a Legislature or other competent authority in the territory of India before the commencement of this Constitution and not previously repealed, not withstanding that any such law or any part thereof may not be then in operation either at all or in particular areas.
 (4) Nothing in this Article shall apply to any amendment of this Constituion made under Article 368.
39. *Surpa* note 37.
40. *Ibid.*
41. *Ibid.*
42. *Ibid.*
43. *Ibid.*
44. Sharma, G.S., *Changing Perceptions of Law in India*, JLJ Vol. VII (1967) p. 2.
45. Law in Changing Society (1972) p. 503.
46. *Connect*, UNESCO-UNEP Environmental Education Newsletter, Vol. XVIII No. 1, March 1993, p. 4.
47. Jariwala C.M., *Direction of Environmental Justice in India: Critical Appraisal of 1987 Case Law*. 35 JILI, 1993 p. 101.

APENDIX A

RULES FOR THE MANUFACTURE, USE, IMPORT, EXPORT AND STORAGE OF HAZARDOUS MICRO-ORGANISMS/ GENETICALLY ENGINEERED ORGANISMS OR CELLS

Notification No. G.S.R.1037 (E), dated December 5, 1989

In exercise of the powers conferred by Sections 6, 8 and 25 of the Environment (Protection) Act, 1986 (29 of 1986) and with a view of protection the environment, nature and health, in connection with the application of gene technology and micro-organisms, the Central Government hereby makes the following rules, namely:

1. Short Title, Extent and Commencement

(1) These rules may be called the Rules for the manufacture, use, import, export and storage of hazardous micro-organisms/genetically engineered organisms or cells.

(2) These rules shall come into operation on the date to be notified for this purpose in the Official Gazette.

2. Application

(1) These rules are applicable to the manufacture, import and storage of micro-organisms and gene-technological products.

(2) These rules shall apply to genetically engineered organisms/micro-organisms and cells and correspondingly to any substances and products and food and stuffs, etc., of which such cells, organisms or tissues hereof form part.

(3) These rules shall also apply to new gene-technologies apart from those referred to in clauses (ii) and (iv) of rule 3 and these rules shall apply to organisms/micro-organisms and cells generated by the utilisation of such other gene-technologies and to substances and products of which such organisms and cells form part.

(4) These rules shall be applicable in the following specific cases:

(a) Sale, offers for sale, storage for the purpose of sale, offers and any kind of handling over with or without a consideration;

(b) exportation and importation of genetically engineered cells or organisms;

(c) production, manufacturing, processing, storage, import drawing off, packaging and repackaging of the genetically engineered products;

(d) production manufacture etc. of drugs and pharmaceuticals and food stuffs, distilleries and tanneries, etc., which make use of micro organisms/genetically engineered micro-organisms one way or the other.

(5) These rules shall be applicable to the whole of India.

3. Definition

In these rules, unless the context requires,

(i) "Bio-technology" means the application of scientific and engineering principles to the processing of materials by biological agents to produce goods and services;

(ii) "Cell hybridisation" means the formation of live cells with new combinations of genetic material through the fusion of two or more cells by means of methods which do not occur naturally;

(iii) "Gene Technology" means the application of the gene technique called genetic engineering, including self cloning and deletion as well as cell hybridisation;

(iv) "Genetic engineering" means the technique by which heritable material which does not usually occur or will not occur naturally in the organisms or cell concerned, generated outside the organism or the cell is inserted into said cell or organism. It shall also mean the formation of new combinations or genetic material by incorporation of a cell into a host cell, where they occur naturally (self cloning) as well as modification of an organism or in a cell by deletion and removal of parts of the heritable material;

(v) "Micro-organisms" shall include all the bacteria, viruses, fungi, mycoplasma, cell lines, algae, protozoans and nematodes indicated in the schedule and those that have not been presently known to exist in the country.

4. Competent Authorities

(1) Recombinant DNA Advisory Committee (RDAC)

This committee shall review developments in Biotechnology at national and international levels and shall recommend suitable and appropriate safety regulations for India in recombinant research, use and applications from time to time. The committee shall function in the Department of Biotechnology.

(2) Review Committee on Genetic Manipulation (RCGM)

This committee shall function in the Department of Biotechnology to monitor the safety related aspects in respect of on-going research projects and activities involving genetically engineered organisms/ hazardous micro-organisms. The Review Committee on Genetic Manipulation shall include representatives of (a) Department of Biotechnology (b) Indian Council of Medical Research (c) Indian Council of Agricultural Research (d) Council of Scientific and Industrial Research (e) other experts in their individual capacity. Review Committee on Genetic Manipulation may appoint sub groups.

It shall bring out manuals of guidelines specifying procedure for regulatory process with respect to activities involving genetically engineered organisms in research, use and applications, including industry, with a view to ensure environmental safety. All ongoing projects involving high risk category and controlled field experiments shall be reviewed to ensure that adequate precautions and containment conditions are followed as per the guidelines.

The Review Committee on Genetic Manipulation shall lay down procedures restricting or prohibiting production, sale, importation and use of such genetically engineered organisms or cells as are mentioned in the schedule.

(3) Institutional Biosafety Committee (IBSC)

This committee shall be constituted by an occupier or any person, including research institutions, handling micro-organisms/ genetically engineered organisms. The committee shall comprise the Head of the Institution, scientists engaged in DNA work, a medical expert and a nominee of the Department of Biotechnology. The occupier or any person including research institutions handling micro-organisms/genetically engineered organisms shall prepare, with the assistance of the Institutional Bio-safety Committee (IBSC) an up-to-date on-site emergency plan according to the manuals/guidelines of the RCGM and make available copies to the District Level Committee/State Biotechnology Co-ordination Committee and the Genetic Engineering Approval Committee.

(4) Genetic Engineering Approval Committee (GEAC)

This committee shall function as a body under the Department of Environment, Forests and Wildlife for approval of activities involving large scale use of hazardous micro-organisms and recombinants in research and industrial production from the environmental angle. The Committee shall also be responsible for approval of proposals relating to release of genetically engineered organisms and products into the environment, including experimental field trials.

(5) State Biotechnology Co-ordination Committee (SBCC)

There shall be a State Biotechnology Co-ordination Committee in the States wherever necessary. It shall have powers to inspect, investigate and take punitive action in case of violation of statutory provisions through the Nodal Department and the State Pollution Control Board/ Directorate of Health/Medical Services. The Committee shall review periodically the safety and control measures in the various industries/ institutions handling genetically engineered organisms/hazardous micro-organisms.

(6) District Level Committee (DLC)

There shall be a District Level Biotechnology Committee (DLC) in the districts wherever necessary under the District Collectors to monitor the safety regulations in installations engaged in the use of genetically modified organisms/hazardous micro-organisms and its applications in the environment.

The District Level Committee or any other persons authorised in this behalf shall visit the installation engaged in activity involving genetically engineered organisms, hazardous micro-organisms, formulate an information chart, find out hazards & risks associated with each of these installations & co-ordinate activities with a view to meeting any emergency. They shall also prepare an off-site emergency plan. The District Level Committee shall regularly submit its report to the State Biotechnology Co-ordination Committee and the Genetic Engineering Approval Committee.

5. Classification of Micro-organisms or Genetically Engineered Product:

(1) For the purpose of these rules, micro-organisms or genetically engineered organisms, products or cells shall be dealt with under two major heads; animal pathogens and plant pests and these shall be classified in the manner specified in the schedule.

(2) If any of the micro-organisms/genetically engineered organisms or cell falls within the limits of more than risk class as specified in the schedule, it shall be deemed to belong exclusively to the last in number of such classes.

6. Micro-organisms laid down in the Schedule are Divided into the following:

(i) Bacterial Agents;
(ii) Fungal Agents;
(iii) Parasitic Agents;
(iv) Viral, Rickettsial and Chlamydial Agents;
(v) Special Category.

7. Approval and Prohibition, etc.:

(1) No person shall import, export, transport, manufacture, process, use or sell any hazardous micro-organism or genetically engineered organism/ substance or cell except with the approval of the Genetic Engineering Approval Committee.

(2) Use of pathogenic micro-organisms or any genetically engineered organism or cell for the purpose of research shall only be allowed in laboratories or inside laboratory areas notified by the Ministry of Environment and Forests for this purpose under the Environment (Protection) Act, 1986.

(3) The Genetic Engineering Approval Committee shall give directions to the occupier to determine or take measures concerning the discharge of micro-organisms/genetically engineered organisms or

cells mentioned in the schedule from the laboratories, hospitals and other areas including prohibition of such discharges and laying down measures to be taken to prevent such discharges.

(4) Any person operating or using genetically engineered organisms/ micro-organisms mentioned in the schedule for scale up or pilot operations shall have to obtain license issued by the Genetic Engineering Approval Committee for any such activity. The possessor shall have to apply for licence in the prescribed proforma.

(5) Certain experiments for the purpose of education within the field of gene technology or micro-organism may be carried outside the laboratories and laboratory areas mentioned in sub-rule (2) and will be looked after by the Institutional Biosafety Committee.

8. Production

Production in which genetically engineered organisms or cells or micro-organisms are generated or used shall not be commenced except with the consent of Genetic Engineering Approval Committee with respect to the discharge of genetically engineered organisms or cells into the environment. This shall also apply to production taking place in connection with development, testing and experiments where such production etc. is not subject to rule 7.

9. Deliberate or Unintentional Release

(1) Deliberate or unintentional release of genetically engineered organisms/hazardous micro-organisms or cells, including deliberate release for the purpose of experiment shall not be allowed.
Note: Deliberate release shall mean any intentional transfer of genetically engineered organisms/hazardous micro-organisms or cells to the environment or nature, irrespective of the way in which it is done.

(2) The Genetic Engineering Approval Committee may in special cases give approval of deliberate release.

10. Permission and Approval for Certain Substances

Substances and products, which contain genetically engineered organisms or cells or micro-organisms shall not be produced, sold, imported or used except with the approval of the Genetic Engineering Approval Committee.

11. Permission and Approval for Food Stuffs

Food stuffs, ingredients in food stuffs and additives, including processing aids, containing or consisting of genetically engineered organisms or cells, shall not be produced, sold, imported or used except with the approval of the Genetic Engineering Approval Committee.

12. Guidelines

(1) Any person who applies for approval under rules 8–11 shall, as determined by the Genetic Engineering Approval Committee submit information and make examinations or cause examinations to be made to elucidate the case, including examinations according to specific directions and at specific laboratories. He shall also make available an on-site emergency plan to the Genetic Engineering Approval Committee before obtaining the approval. If the authority itself makes an examination, it may order the applicant to defray the expenses incurred by it in doing so.

(2) Any person to whom an approval has been granted under rules 8–11 above shall notify the Genetic Engineering Approval Committee of any change in or addition to information already submitted.

13. Grant of Approval

(1) In connection with the granting of approval under rules 8 to 11 above, terms and conditions shall be stipulated, including terms and conditions as to the control to be exercised by the applicant, supervisions, restriction on use, the layout of the enterprise as to the submission of information to the State Biotechnology Co-ordination Committee or to the District Level Committee.

(2) All approvals of the Genetic Engineering Approval Committee shall be for a specified period not exceeding four years at the first instance renewable for 2 years at a time. The Genetic Engineering Approval Committee shall have powers to revoke such approval in the following situations:

(a) if there is any new information as to the harmful effects of the genetically engineered organisms or cells;

(b) if the genetically engineered organisms or cells cause such damage to the environment, nature or health as could not be envisaged when the approval was given; or

(c) non-compliance of any condition stipulated by the Genetic Engineering Approval Committee.

14. Supervision

(1) The Genetic Engineering Approval Committee may supervise the implementation of the terms and conditions laid down in connection with the approvals accorded by it.

(2) The Genetic Engineering Approval Committee may carry out this supervision through the State Biotechnology Co-ordination Committee or the State Pollution Control Board/District Level Committee or through any person authorised in this behalf.

15. Penalties

(1) If an order is not complied with, the District Level Committee or State Biotechnology Co-ordination Committee may take measures at the expense of the person who is responsible.

(2) In case where immediate intervention is required in order to prevent any damage to the environment, nature or health, the District Level Committee or State Biotechnology Co-ordination Committee may take the necessary steps without issuing any orders or notice. The expenses incurred for this purpose will be repayable by the person responsible for such damage.

(3) The State Biotechnology Co-ordination Committee/District Level Committee may take samples for a more detailed examination of organisms and cells.

(4) The State Biotechnology Co-ordination Committee/District Level Committee shall be competent to ask for assistance from any other Government authority to carry out its instructions.

16. Responsibility to Notify Interruption or Accidents

(1) Any person who under rules 7–11 is responsible for conditions or arrangements shall immediately notify the District Level Committee, State Bio-technology Co-ordination Committee and the state medical officer of any interruption of operations or accidents that

may lead to discharge of genetically engineered organisms or cells which may be harmful to the environment, nature of health or involve any danger thereto.

(2) Any notice given under sub-rule (1) above shall not lessen the duty of the person who is responsible to try effectively to minimise or prevent the effects of interruption of operations or accidents.

17. Preparation of Off-site Emergency Plan by the DLC

(1) It shall be the duty of the DLC to prepare an off-site emergency plan detailing how emergencies relating to a possible major accident at a site will be dealt with and in preparing the plan, the DLC shall consult the occupier and such other person as it may deem necessary.

(2) For the purpose of enabling the DLC to prepare the emergency plan required under sub-rule (1), the occupier shall provide the DLC with such information relating to the handling of hazardous micro-organisms/genetically engineered organisms under his control as the DLC may require, including the nature, extent and likely off-site effects of a possible major accident and the DLC shall provide the occupier with any information from the off-site emergency plan which relates to his duties under rule 16.

18. Inspection and Information Regarding Finance

(1) The State Biotechnology Co-ordination Committee or the Genetic Engineering Approval Committee/ the DLC or any person with special knowledge duly authorised by the State Biotechnology Co-ordination Committee or the Genetic Engineering Approval Committee or the DLC where it is deemed necessary, at any time on due production of identity be admitted to public as well as to private premises and localities for the purpose of carrying out supervision.

(2) Any person who is responsible for activities subject to rules 7–11 above shall at the request of District Level Committee or State Biotechnology Co-ordination Committee or the Genetic Engineering Approval Committee submit all such information, including information relating to financial conditions and accounts, as is essential to the authority's administration under these rules. He shall also allow supervision or inspection by the authorities or persons indicated in sub-rule.(1).

[SCHEDULE]

A. ANIMAL AND HUMAN PATHOGENS

(3) The Genetic Engineering Approval Committee may fix fees to cover, in whole or in part, the expenses incurred by the authorities in connection with approvals, examinations, supervision and control.

19. Appeal

(1) Any person aggrieved by a decision made by the Genetic Engineering Approval Committee/State Biotechnology Co-ordination Committee in pursuance of these rules may within thirty days from the date on which the decision is communicated to him, prefer an appeal to such authority as may be appointed by the Ministry of Environment and Forests provided that the Appellate Authority may entertain the appeal after the expiry of the said period of thirty days if such authority is satisfied that the appellant was prevented by sufficient cause from filing the appeal in time.

20. Exemption

The Ministry of Environment and Forests shall, wherever necessary, exempt an occupier handling a particular micro-organism/genetically engineered organism from rules 7–11.

BACTERIAL

Risk Group II

Acinetobacter calcoacetieus
Actinobacillus—all species except A mallei, which is in Risk Group III
Aeromonoas hydrophila
Arizona hinshawii-all serotypes
Bacillus anthracis
Bordetella—all species
Borrelia recurrentis, B. vincenti
Campylobacter fetus
Camphylobacter jejuni
Chalamydia psittaci
Cheamydia trachomatis
Clostridium chauvoei. Cl. difficile Cl, fallax, Clhaemolyticum Cl histolyticum, Cl. novyi, (Cl. perfringes), Cl. speticum, Cl. sordelli
Corynebacterium diptheriae, C. equi, C. haemolyticum, C. pseudotuberculosis, C. pyogenes, C. renale
Diplococcus (Streptococcus) pneumoniae Edwardsiila tarda

Moraxella—all species
Mycobateria—all species including Mycobacterium avium
M. Bovis, M. tuberculosis,
M. leprae
Mycoplasma—all species except
M. mycoides and M. angalactiae
Neisseric gonorrhoea, N. meningitis
Pasteruella—all species ecxept those listed in Risk Group III
Salmonella—all species and all serotypes Sphaerophorus
Shigella—all species and all serotypes necrophorus
Staphylococcus aureus
Streptobacillus moniliformis
Streptococcus pneumoniae
Streptococcus pyogenes, S. equi
Streptomyces madurae, S. pelleteri, S. somaliensls
Treponema carateum, T. pallidum and T. pertenue
Vibrio foetus, V. comma including biotype EL Tor and V. parahemolyticus.
Vibrio cholerae

Risk Group III

Antinobacillus mallei
Bartonella—all species
Brucella—all species
Clostridium botulium, Cl. tetani
Francisella tularensis
Erysipelothix insidiosa
Escherichia Coli—all enteropathogenic serotypes, enterotoxigenic
Haemophilus ducrevi, H. influenzae, H. pneumoniae
Herellea vaginicola
Klebsiella—all species & all serotypes
Legionella pneumophila
Letionella
Leptospira interrogans—all serotypes reported in India
Listeria, all species Mima polymorpha

FUNGAL

Risk Group II

Antinomycetes (including Nocardia SP, (Antinomyces species and Arachina propinica)
Aspergillus fumigatus
Blastomyces dermatitis
Cryptococcus neoformans
C. fersiminosos
Epidermophyton madurella, microsporon
Paracoccidioides brasiliensis
Sporothrix
Trichoderma
Trichophyton

Risk Group III

Coccidiodes immitis
Histoplasma capulatum
Histoplasma capsulatum var duboissi

PARASITIC

Risk Group II

Entamoeba histolytica
Leishmania species
Naegleria gruberia
Plasmodium theilera; P. babesia, P. falcoparum
Plasmodium babesia
Schistosoma
Toxoplasma gondii
Mycobacterium avium, M. bovis, M. tuberculosis. M. leprae
Pasteurella multocid type B ("buffalo" and other foreign virulent strains)
Pseudomonas pseudomallai
Yersinia pestis
Encephalomyocarditis virus. (EMC)
Flanders virus
Hart Part virus
Hepatitis—associated antigen material hepatitis A and B viruses, non A and non B, HDV
Herpes viruses—expect herpesvirus simiae (monkey B virus) which is in Risk Group IV.
Infectious Bovine Rhinotraechitis virus (IBR)
Infectious Bursal diseases of poultry & Infectious Bronchitus
Infectious Laryngotraechitis (ILT)
Influenza virus—all types, except A/PR8/34 which is in Risk Group I
Langat virus Leucosis Complex
Lymphogranuloma venereum agent
Marek's Disease virus
Measles virus
Mumps virus
New castle Disease virus (other than licenced strain for vaccine use)
Parainfluenza viruses—all types except parainfluenza virus, 3, SF4 strain, which is in Risk Group I.
Polio viruses—all types, wild and attenuated
Poxviruses—all types except, Alastrim, monkey pox, sheep pox and white pox, which depending on experiments are in Risk Group III or IV
Rabies virus—all strains except rabies stret virus, which should be classified in Risk Group III when inoculated into carnivores.
Reoviruses—all types
Respiratory syncytial virus

Rhinoviruses—all types
Rinderpest-(other than vaccine strain in use)
Rubella virus
Simian viruses—all types except herpeavirus simlae (Monkey Virus) which is in Risk Group IV.
Simian viruses 40
Toxocara canis
Trichinella spiralis
Trichomanas
Trypanosoma cruzi

Risk Group III

Schisistosoma mansoni

VIRAL RICKETTSIAL AND CHLAMYDIAL

Risk Group II

Adenoviruses—Human, all types
Avain loukosis
Cache Valley virus
CELQ (avain adenovirus)
Coxsackie A and B viruses
Corona viruses
Cytomegalo viruses
Dengue virus, when used for transmission experiments
Echo viruses—all types
Turlock virus
Vaccinia virus
Varicella virus
Vole rickettsia
Yellow fever virus, 17D vaccine strain

Risk Group III

African House Sickness (attenuated strain except animal passage)
Alastrim, monkey pox and white pox, when used in vitro
Arboviruses—All strains except those in Risk Groups II and IV
Blue tongue virus (only serotypes reported in India)
Ebola fever virus
Epstein-Barr virus
Feline Leukemia
Feline sarvoma
Foot and Mouth Disease viruse (all serotypes and subtypes)
Gibbon Ape Lymphosarcoma
Herpesvirus ateles
Ad 7 SV 40 (defective)
Sindbis virus
Tensaw virus

Risk Group IV

Alastrim, monkey pox, whitepox, when used for transmission or animal
inoculation experiments
Hemorrhagic fever agents, including Crimean hemorrhagic gever (congo)
Korean hemorrhagic fever
and others as yet undefined
Herpesvirus simlae (monkey B virus)

Tick-borne encephalitis virus complex, including- Russion Spring Summar Encephalitis, Kyasanur Forest Disease, omsk hemorrhagic fever and Central Euro pean encephalitis viruses.

SPECIAL CATEGORY BACTERIAL

Contagious Equine Metritis (H. equigenitalis)
Pestisc petit de ruminantium

VIRAL RICKETTSIAL AND CHLAMYDIAL

African Horse Sickness virus (serotypes not reported in India & challenge strains)
African Swine Fever
Bat rabies virus
Blue tongue virus (serotypes not reported in India)
Exoitic FED virus types & sub-types
Junin and Machupo viruses
Lassa virus
Marburg virus
Murrey valley encephalitis virus
Rift Valley Fever virus
Smallpox virus—Archieval storage and propagation Swine
Vesicular Disease
Veneseulan equine encephalitis virus
Yellow fever virus-Wild strain
Other Arboviruses causing epizootics and so far not recorded in India
Herpesvirus saimiri
Herpes simplex 2
HIV-1 & HIV-2 and strains of SIV
Infectious Equine Anaemia
Lymphocytic choriomeningitis cirus (LCM)
Monkey pox, when used in vitro
Non-defective Adeno-2 SV-40 hydrids
Psittacosis-ornithosis-trachoma group of agents
Pseudorabies virus
Rabies street virus, when used in inoculations of carnivores
Rickettsia—all species except Vole rickettsia and Coxiell purnetti when used for
vector transmission or animal inoculation experiments
Sheep pox (field strain)
Swine Fever virus
Vesicular stomatitis virus
Wolly monkey Fibrosarcoma
Yaba pox virus

B. PLANT PESTS

Any living stage (including active and dormant forms) of insects, mites, nematodes, slugs, snails, bacteria, fungi, protozoa, other parasitic plants or productive parts thereof: viruses; or any organisms similar to or allied with any of the foregoing; or any infectious agents or substances, which can directly or indirectly injure or cause disease or damage in or to any plants or parts thereof, or any processed, manufactured, or other products of plants are considered plant pests.

Organisms belonging to all lower Taxa contained within the group listed are also included.

1. Viruses

All viroids

All bacterial, fungal algal, plant insect & nematode viruses; special care should be taken for—

- (i) Geminiviruses,
- (ii) Caulimoviruses,
- (iii) Nuclear Polyhedrosis viruses,
- (iv) Granulosis viruses, and
- (v) Cytoplasmic polyhedrosis viruses,

2. Bacteria

Family Pseudomonadaceae
- Genus Pseudomonas
- Genus Xanthomonas
- Genus Azotobacter

Family Rhizobiaceae
- Genus Rhizobium
- Azorhizobium
- Genus Bradyrhizobium
- Genus Agrobacterium
- Genus Phyllobacterium
- Genus Erwinia
- Genus Enterobacter
- Genus Klebzieller

Family Spirollaceae
- Genus Azospirillum
- Genus Acquspirillum
- Genus Oceonospirillum

Family Streptomycetaceae
- Genus Streptomyces
- Genus Noerdia

Family Rickettsiacceae
- Rickettsial-like organims associated with insect diseases
- Gram-nagative phloem-limited bacteria associated with plant disease
- Gram-negative xylem-limited bacteria associated with plant diseases

Cyanobacteria—All members of blue-green algae

Mollicutes

Family Spiroplasmataceae

Mycoplasma-like organisms associated with plant diseases
Mycoplasma-like organisms associated with insect diseases

Algae

Family Chnolophyceae
Family Euglenophyceae
Family Pyrophyceae
Family Chrysophyceae
Family Phaephyceae
Family Rhodophyceae
Family Plasmodiophoraceae
Family Chytridiaceae
Family Olpidiopsidaceae
Family Synchytriaceae
Family Gatenariaceae
Family Coelomomycetaceae
Family Saprolegniaceae
Family Zoopagaceae
Family Albuginiaceae
Family Peronosporaceae
Family Pythiaceae
Family Mucoraceae
Family Choanephoraceae
Family Mortiercllaceae
Family Actinomycetaceae
Genus Actinomyces
Coryneform Group
Genus Clavibacter
Genus Arthrobacter
Genus Curtobacterium
Genus Bdellovibro
Family Endogonaceae
Family Syncephalastraceae
Family Dimargaritaceae
Family Kickxellaceae
Family Saksenaeceae
Family Entomophthoraceae
Family Ecerinaceae
Family Taphrinaceae
Family Endomycetaceae
Family Saccharomycetaceae
Family Eurotiaceae
Family Gymnoascaceae
Family Aseophaeriaceae
Family Onygenaceae
Family Microascaceae
Family Protomycetaceae
Family Elsinoeaceae
Family Myriangiaceae
Family Dothidiaceae
Family Chaetothyriaceae
Family Parmulariaceae
Family Phillipsiellaceae
Family Hysteriaceae
Family Pleosporaceae
Family Melamomataceae
Family Ophiostomataceae
Family Aseophaeriaceae
Family Erysiphaceae
Family Meliolaceae
Family Xylariaceae
Family Diaporthaceae
Family Hypoereaceae
Family Clavicipataceae
Family Phacidiaceae
Family Ascocorticiaceae
Family Hemiphacidiaceae
Family Dermateceae
Family Sclerotiniaceae
Family Cyttariaceae
Family Helosiaceae
Family Sarcostomataceae
Family Sarcoscyphaceae
Family Auricolariaceae
Family Ceratobasidiaceae

Family Corticiaceae
Family Polyporaceae
Family Tricholomataceae
Family Ustilaginaceae
Family Sporbolomycetaceae
Family Uredinaceae
Family Agricaceae
Family Grpahiolaceae
Family Pucciniaceae
Family Melampsoraceae
Family Gandodermataceae
Family Labonlbeniaceae
Family Sphaeropsidaceae
Family Melabconiaceae
Family Dematiaceae
Family Moniliaceae
Family Aganomucetaceae

Parasitic Weeds

Family Balanophoraceae—parasitic species
Family Cuscutaceae—parasitic species
Family Ttydonoraceae—parasitic species
Family Lauraceae—parasitic species
Genus Cassytha
Family Lennoaceae—parasitic species
Family Loranthaceae—parasitic species
Family Myzodendraceae—parasitic species
Family Olacaceae—parasitic species
Family Orobanchaceae—parasitic species
Family Rafflesiaceae—parasitic species
Family Santalaceae—parasitic species
Family Scrophulariaceae—parasitic species

Protozoa

Genus Phytomonas
And all Protozoa associated with insect diseases.

Nematodes

Family Anguinidae
Family Belonolaimidae
Family Caloosiidae
Family Criconematidae
Family Dolichodoridae
Family Fergusobiidae
Family Hemicycliophoridae
Family Heteroderidae
Family Hoplolaimidae
Superfamily Careoidea
Superfamily Pentatomoidea
Superfamily Pyrrhocoroidea
Family Hymenochaetaceae
Family Echinodintiaceae
Family Eistuliniaceae
Family Clavaraceae
Family Meloidgynidae
Family Neotylenchidae
Family Nothotylenchidae
Family Paratylenchidae
Family Pratylenchidae
Family Tylenchidae
Family Tylenchulidae
Family Aphelenchoidiae

Family Longidoridae
Family Trichodoridae

Mollusca

Superfamily Planorbacea
Superfamily Achatinacea
Superfamily Arionacea
Superfamily Limacacea
Superfamily Helicacea
Superfamily Veronicellacea

Arthropoda

Superfamily Ascoidea
Superfamily Dermanyssoidea
Superfamily Erjophyoidea
Superfamily Teranychoidea
Superfamily Eupodoidea
Superfamily Tydeoidea
Superfamily Erythraenoidea
Superfamily Trombidioidea
Superfamily Hydryphantoidea
Superfamily Tarasonemoidea
Superfamily Pyemotoidea
Superfamily Hemisarcoptoidea
Superfamily Acaroidea
Order Polydesmida
Family Sminthoridea
Family Forfieulidae
Order Isoptera
Order Thysanoptera
Family Acrididea
Family Gryllidea
Family Gryllacrididae
Family Gryllotalpidae
Family Phasmatidae
Family Ronaleidae
Family Tettigoniidae
Family Tetragidae
Family Thaumastocoridae
Superfamily Piesmatoidea
Superfamily Lygaeoidea
Superfamily Idiostoloidea
Family Sircidae
Family Tenthredinidae
Superfamily Tingoidea
Superfamily Miroidea
Order Homoptera
Family Anobiidae
Family Byturidae
Family Cantharidae
Family Carabidae
Family Ceambycidae
Family Chrysomelidae
Family Coecinellidae
Family Curculionidae
Family Dermestidae
Family Elateridae
Family Hydrophilidae
Family Lyctidae
Family Meloidae
Family Mordellidae
Family Platypodidae
Family Scarabaeldae
Family Scolytidae
Family Selbytidae
Order Lepidoptera
Family Agromyzidae
Family Anthomiidae
Family Cecidomiidae
Family Chioropidae
Family Ephydridae
Family Lonchaeidae
Family Muscidae
Family Otitidae
Family Syrphidae
Family Tephritidae

Family Tipulidae
Family Apideae
Family Caphidae
Family Chalcidae
Family Cynipidae
Family Eurytomidae
Family Formicidae
Family Psilidae
Family Torymidae
Family Xyloiopidae
and

Also unclassified organisms and/or organisms whose classification is unknown, and all other organisms associated with plant & insect diseases.

MINISTRY OF ENVIRONMENT & FORESTS

(Department of Environment, Forests & Wildlife)

Notification under Section 3(1) and Section 3(2)(v) of the Environment (Protection) Act, 1986 & Rule 5(3)(d) of Environment (Protection) Rules, 1986 Declaring Coastal Stretches as Coastal Regulation Zone (CRZ) and Regulating Activities in the CRZ.

New Delhi, the 19th February 1991.

S.O. 114(E) - Whereas a Notification under Sec. 3(1) and Sec. 3(2)(v) of the Environment (Protection) Act, 1986, inviting objections against the declaration of Coastal Stretches as Coastal Regulations Zone (CRZ) and imposing restriction on industries, operations and processes in the CRZ was published vide S.O.No. 944 (E) dated 15th December 1990.

And whereas all objections received have been duly considered by the Central Government;

Now, therefore, in exercise of the powers conferred by Clause (d) of sub-rule (3) of Rule 5 of the Environment (Protection) Rules, 1986, and all other powers vesting in its behalf, the Central Government hereby declared the Coastal Stretches of seas, bays, estuaries, creeks, rivers and backwaters which are influenced by tidal action (in the landward side) upto 500 meters from the High Tide Line (HTL) and the land between the Low Tide Line (LTL) and the HTL as Coastal Regulation Zone and imposes with effect from the date of this Notification, the following restrictions of the setting up and expansion of industry, operations or processes etc. in the said Coastal Regulation Zone (CRZ). For Purposes of this Notification, the High Tide Line (HTL) will be defined as the line upto which the highest high tide reaches during spring tides.

Note: The distance from the High Tide Line (HTL) to which the proposed regulations will apply in the case of rivers, creeks and backwaters may be modified on a case by case basis for reasons to be recorded while preparing the Coastal Zone Management Plans (referred to below); however, this distance will not be less than 100 meters or the width of the creek, river or backwater, whichever is less.

2. Prohibited Activities

The following activities are declared as prohibited within the Coastal Regulation Zone, namely:

(i) setting up of new industries and expansion of existing industries, except those directly related to the waterfront or directly needing foreshore facilities;

(ii) manufacture or handling or storage or disposal of hazardous substances as specified in the Notifications of the Government of India in the Ministry of Environment and Forests No. S.O. 594 (E) dated 28th July 1989, S.O. 966 (E) dated 27th November 1989 and G.S.R. 1037 (E) dated 5th December 1989.

(iii) setting up and expansion of fish processing units including warehousing (excluding hatchery and natural fish drying in permitted areas);

(iv) setting up and expansion of units, mechanisms for disposal of wastes and effluents, except facilities required for discharging treated effluents into the water course with approval under the Water (Prevention and Control of Pollution) Act, 1974 except for storm water drains.

(v) discharge of untreated wastes and effluents from industries, cities or towns and other human settlements. Schemes shall be implemented by the concerned authorities for phasing out the existing practices, if any, within a reasonable time period not exceeding three years from the date of this notification;

(vi) dumping of city or town waste for the purpose of land filling or otherwise; the existing practices, if any, shall be phased out within a reasonable time not exceeding three years from the date of this notification;

(vii) dumping of ash or any wastes from thermal power stations;

(viii) land reclamation, bunding or disturbing the natural course of sea water with similar obstructions except those required for control of coastal erosion and maintenance or cleaning of waterways, channels and ports and for prevention of sand bars and also, except for tidal regulators, storm water drains and structures for prevention of salinity ingress and for sweet water recharge;

(ix) mining of land, rocks and other substrata materials except those rare minerals not available outside CRZ areas;

(x) harvesting or drawal of ground waters and construction of mechanisms therefore within 200 m of HTL; in the 200 m or 500 m zones. It shall be permitted only when done manually through ordinary wells for drinking, horticulture, agriculture and fisheries;

(xi) construction activities in ecologically sensitive areas as specified in Annexure-I of this notification;

(xii) any construction activity between the Low Tide Line and High Tide Line except facilities or carrying treated effluents and waste water discharges into the sea, facilities for carrying sea water for cooling purposes, oil, gas and similar pipelines and facilities essential for activities permitted under this notification; and

(xiii) dressing or altering of sand dunes, hills, natural features including landscape changes for beautification, recreational and other such purpose, except as permissible under this notification;

3. Regulation of Permissible Activities

All other activities except those prohibited in para 2 above, will be regulated as under:

(i) Clearance shall be given for any activity within the Coastal Regulation Zone only if it requires waterfront and foreshore facilities;

(ii) The following activities will require environmental clearance from the Ministry of Environment and Forest, Government of India, namely:

(a) Construction activities related to defence requirements for which foreshore facilities are essential (e.g. slipways, jetties etc.); except for classified operational component of defence projects for which a separate procedure shall be followed. (Residental buildings, office buildings, hospital complexes, workshops shall not come within the definition of operational requirements except in very special cases and hence shall not normally be permitted on the C.R.Z.)

(b) Operational constructions for ports and hardours and light-houses requiring water frontage; jetties, wharfs, quays, slipways etc. (Residental buildings and office buildings shall not come within the definition of operational activities except in very special cases and hence shall not normally be permitted in the C.R.Z.)

(c) Thermal power plants (only foreshore facilities for transport of raw materials, facilities for intake of cooling water and outfall for discharge of treated waste water/cooling water); and

(d) All other activities with investment exceeding Rs. 5 corers.

(iii) (a) The coastal states and Union Territory administrations shall prepare, within a period of one year from the date of this notification, coastal Zone Management Plants identifying and classifying the CRZ areas within their respective territories in accordance with the guidelines given in Annexures I and II of the notification and obtain approval (with or without modifications) of the Central Government in the Ministry of Environment and Forests;

(b) Within the framework of such approved plans all development and activities within the CRZ other than those covered in para 2 and para 3(2) above shall be regulated by the State Government, Union Territory administration or the local authority as the case may be in accordance with the guidelines given in Annexures I and II of the notification; and

(c) In the interim period till the Coastal Zone Management Plans mentioned in para 3(3) (i) above are prepared and approved, all developments and activities within the CRZ shall not violate the provisions of this notification. State Government and Union Territory administrations shall ensure adherence to these regulations and violations, if any, shall be subjected to the provisions of the Environment (Protection) Act, 1986.

4. Procedure of Monitoring and Enforcement

The Ministry of Environment and Forests and the Government of State or Union Territory and such other authorities at the State or Union Territory level, as may be designated for this purpose shall be responsible for monitoring and enforcement of the provisions of the Notifications within their respective jurisdictions.

[N.K-15019/1/84-1A-III (Vol. II)]

R. Rajamani, Secy.

ANNEXURE
COASTAL AREA CLASSIFICATION AND DEVELOPMENT REGULATIONS

Classification of Coastal Regulation Zone

6(1) For regulating development activities, the coastal stretches within 500 mts. of the High Tide Line of the landward side are classified into 4 categories, namely:

Category I (CRZ-I):

(i) Areas that are ecologically sensitive and important, such as national parks/marine parks, sanctuaries, reserve forests, wildlife habitats, mangroves, corals/coral reefs, areas close to breeding and spawning grounds of fish and other marine life, areas of outstanding natural beauty/historical/ heritage areas, areas rich in genetic diversity, areas likely to be innundated due to rising sea level consequent upon global warming and such other areas as may be declared by the Central Government or the concerned authorities at the State/Union Territory level from time to time.

(ii) Area between Low Tide Line and the High Tide line.

Category II (CRZ-II):

The areas that have already been developed upto or close to the shoreline. For this purpose, developed area is referred to as that area within the municipal limits or is other legally designated urban areas which is already substantially built up and which has been provided with drainage and approach roads and other infra-structural facilities such as water supply and sewerage mains.

Category III (CRZ-III):

Areas that are relatively undisturbed and those which do not belong to either Category I or II. These include coastal zones in the rural areas (developed and undeveloped) and also areas within municipal limits or in other legally designated urban areas which are not substantially built up.

Category IV (CRZ-IV):

Coastal stretches in the Andaman & Nicobar, Lakshadweep and small islands except those designated as CRZ-I, CRZ-II or CRZ-III.

Norms for Regulation of Activities

6(2): The development or construction activities in different categories of CRZ areas shall be regulated by the concerned authorities at the State/ Union Territory level in accordance with the following norms:

CRZ-I

No new construction shall be permitted within 500 meters of the High Tide Line. No construction activity, except as listed under 2(xii), will be permitted between the Low Tide Line and the High Tide Line.

CRZ-II

(i) Buildings shall be permitted neither on the seaward side of the existing roads (or roads proposed in the approved Coastal Zone Management Plan of the area) nor on seaward side of existing authorised structures. Buildings permitted on the landward side of the existing and proposed roads/existing authorised structures shall be subjected to the existing local Town and Country Planning Regulations including the existing norms of FSI/FAR.

(ii) Reconstruction of the authorised buildings to be permitted subject to the existing FSI/FAR norms and without change in the existing use.

(iii) The design and construction of buildings shall be consistent with the surrounding landscape and local architectural style.

CRZ-III

(i) The areas upto 200 meters from the High Tide Line is to a be earmarked as 'No Development Zone.' No construction shall be permitted within this zone except for repair of existing authorised structures not exceeding existing FSI, existing plinth area and existing density. However, the following uses may be permissible in this zone—agriculture, horticulture, gardens, pastures, parks, playfields, forestry and salt manufacture from sea water.

(ii) Development of vacant plots between 200 and 500 meters of High Tide Line in designated areas of CRZ-III with prior approval of MEF permitted for construction of hotels/beach resorts for temporary occupation of tourists/visitors subject to the conditions as stipulated in the guidelines in Annexure-II.

(iii) Construction/reconstruction of dwelling units between 200 and 500 metres of the High Tide Line permitted so long as it is within the ambit of traditional rights and customary uses such as existing fishing villages and goathans; building permission for such construction/reconstruction will be subject to conditions that the total number of dwelling units shall not be more than twice the number of existing units; total covered area on all floors shall not exceed 33 per cent of the plot size; the overall height of construction shall not exceed 9 metres and construction shall not be more than 2 floors (ground floor plus one floor).

(iv) Reconstruction/alterations of an existing authorised building permitted subject to (i) to (ii) above.

Andaman & Nicobar Islands:

(i) No new construction of buildings shall be permitted within 200 metres of the HTL;

(ii) The buildings between 200 and 500 metres from the High Tide Line shall not have more than 2 floors (ground floor and 1st floor), the total covered area on all floors shall not be more than 50 percent of the plot size and the total height of construction shall not exceed 9 metres;

(iii) The design and construction of buildings shall be consistent with the surounding landscape and local architectural style;

(iv) Corals and sand from the beaches and coastal waters shall not be used for construction and other purposes;

(v) Dredging and underwater blasting in and around coral formations shall not be permitted; and

(vi) However, in some of the islands, coastal stretches may also be classified into categories CRZ-I or II or III, with the prior approval of the Ministry of Environment and Forests and in such designated stretches, the appropriate regulations given for respective categories shall apply.

Lakshadweep and Small Islands:

(i) For permitting construction of buildings, the distance from the High Tide Line shall be decided depending on the size of the islands. This shall be laid down for each island, in consultation with the experts and with approval of the Ministry of Environment & Forests, keeping in view the land use requirements for specific purposes vis-a-vis local conditions including hydrological aspects, erosion and ecological sensitivity;

(ii) The buildings within 500 metres from the HTL shall not have more than 2 floors (ground floor and 1st floor); the total covered area on all floors shall not be more than 50 per cent of the plot size and the total height of construction shall not exceed 9 metres;

(iii) The design and construction of buildings shall be consistent with the surrounding landscape and local architectural style;

(iv) Corals and sand from the beaches and coastal waters shall not be used for construction and other purposes;

(v) Dredging and underwater blasting in and around coral formations shall not be permitted; and

(vi) However, in some of the islands, costal stretches may also be classified into categories CRZ I or II or III with the prior approval of the Ministry of Environment & Forests and in such designated stretches, the appropriate regulations given for respective categories shall apply.

Guidelines For Development of Beach Resorts/Hotels in the Designated Areas of CRZ-III for Temporary Occupation of Tourists/Visitors, with Prior Approval of the Ministry of Environment & Forests

7(1): Construction of beach resort/hotels with prior approval of MEF in the designated areas of CRZ-III for temporary occupation of tourists/ visitors, shall be subject to the following conditions:

(i) The project proponents shall not undertake any construction (including temporary constructions and fencing or such other barriers) within 200 metres (in the landward side) from the High Tide Line and within the area between the Low Tide and High Tide Line;

(ii) The total plot size shall not be less than 0.4 hectares and the total covered area on all floors shall not exceed 33 per cent of the plot size i.e. the FSI shall not exceed 0.33. The open area shall be suitably landscaped with appropriate vegetal cover;

(iii) The construction shall be consistent with the surrounding landscape and local architectural style;

(iv) The overall height of construction upto the highest ridge of the roof, shall not exceed 9 metres and the construction shall not be more than 2 floors (ground floor plus one upper floor);

(v) Ground water shall not be tapped within 200 m of the HTL; within the 200 metre–500metre zone it can be tapped only with the concurrence of the Central/State Ground Water Board;

(vi) Extraction of sand, levelling or digging of sandy stretches except for structural foundation of building, swimming pool shall not be permitted within 500 metres of the High Tide Line;

(vii) The quality of treated effluents, solid wastes, emission and noise levels etc. from the project area must conform to the standards laid down by the competent authorities, including the Central/State Pollution Control Board and under the Environment (Protection) Act 1986;

(viii) Necessary arrangements for the treatment of the effluents and solid wastes must be made. It must be ensured that the untreated effluents and solid wastes are not discharged into the water or on the beach; and no effluent/solid waste shall be discharged on the beach;

(ix) To allow public access to the beach, atleast a gap of 20 metres width shall be provided between any two hotels/beach resorts; and in no case shall gaps be less than 500 metres apart; and

(x) If the project involves diversion of forest land for non-forest purposes, clearance as required under the Forest (Conservation) Act, 1980 shall be obtained. The requirements of other Central and State laws as applicable to the project shall be met with.

(xi) Approval of the State/Union Territory Tourism Department shall be obtained.

7(2): In ecologically sensitive areas (such as marine parks, mangroves, coral reefs, breeding and spawning grounds of fish, wildlife habitats and such other areas as may be notified by the Central/State Government/Union Territories) construction of beach resorts/hotels shall not be permitted.

APPENDIX C

HAZARDOUS WASTES (MANAGEMENT AND HANDLING) RULES, 1989

Notification No. S.O. 594(E), dated July 28, 1989

In exercise of the powers conferred by Sections 6, 8 and 25 of the Environment (Protection) Act, 1986, (29 of 1986) the Central Government hereby makes the following rules, namely:

1. Short Title & Commencement

(1) These rules may be called the Hazardous Wastes (Management & Handling) Rules, 1989.
(2) They shall come into force on the date of their publication in the Official Gazette.

2. Application

These rules shall apply to hazardous wastes as specified in the Schedule and shall not apply to:

(a) waste water and exhaust gases as covered under the provisions of the Water (Prevention and Control of Pollution) Act, 1974 (6 of 1974), and the Air (Prevention and Control of Pollution) Act, (14 of 1981), and rules made thereunder;
(b) wastes arising out of the operation from ships beyond five kilometers as covered under the provisions of the Merchant Shipping Act, 1958 (44 of 1958), and the rules made thereunder;

(c) radioactive wastes as covered under the provisions of the Atomic Energy Act, 1962 (33 of 1962), and rules made thereunder.

3. Definitions

In these rules unless the context otherwise requires,

(a) 'Act' means the Environment (Protection) Act, 1986 (29 of 1986);
(b) 'applicant' means a person or an organisation that applies, in Form 1, for granting of authorisation to perform specific activities connected with handling of hazardous wastes;
(c) 'authorisation' means permission for collection, reception, treatment, transport, storage and disposal of hazardous wastes, granted by the competent authority in Form 2;
(d) 'authorised person' means a person or an organisation authorised by the competent authority to collect, treat, transport, store or dispose off hazardous wastes in accordance with the guidelines to be issued by the competent authority from time to time;
(e) 'export' with its grammatical variations and cognate expressions, means taking out of India to a place outside India;
(f) 'exporter' means any person under the jurisdiction of the exporting country who exports hazardous wastes and the exporting country itself, which exports hazardous wastes;
(g) 'facility' means any location wherein the process incidental to the waste generation, collection, reception, treatment, storage and disposal are carried out;
(h) 'Form' means form appended to these rules;
(i) 'hazardous wastes' means categories of wastes specified in the Schedule;
(j) 'hazardous wastes sites' means a place for collection, reception, treatment, storage and disposal of hazardous wastes which has been duly approved by the competent authority;
(k) 'import' with its grammatical variations and cognate expressions, means bringing into India from a place outside India;
(l) 'importer' means an occupier or any person who imports hazardous wastes;
(m) 'operator of a facility' means a person who owns or operates a facility for collection, reception, treatment, storage and disposal of hazardous wastes;
(n) 'Schedule' means the Schedule appended to these rules;

(o) 'State Pollution Control Board' means the Board appointed under sub-section (1) of Sec. 4 of the Water (Prevention and Control of Pollution) Act, 1974 (6 of 1974) and under Sec. 4 of the Air (Prevention and Control of Pollution) Act, 1981 (14 of 1981);

(p) 'transboundary movement' means any movement of hazardous wastes or other wastes from an area under the national jurisdiction of one country to or through an area under the national jurisdiction of another country or through an area not under the national jurisdiction of any country, provided at least two countries are involved in the movement;

(q) the words and expressions used in these rules and not defined but defined in the Act, shall have the meanings respectively assigned to them in the Act.

4. Responsibility of the Occupier for Handling of Wastes

(1) The occupier generating hazardous wastes listed in column (2) of the Schedule in quantities equal to or exceeding the limits given in column (3) of the said Schedule, shall take all practical steps to ensure that such wastes are properly handled and disposed off without any adverse effects which may result from such wastes and the occupier shall also be responsible for proper collection, reception, treatment, storage and disposal of these wastes either himself or through the operator of a facility.

(2) The occupier or any other person acting on his behalf who intends to get his hazardous wastes treated by the operator of a facility under sub-rule (1) shall give to the operator of a facility such information as may be specified by the State Pollution Control Board.

5. Grant of Authorisation for Handling Hazardous Wastes

(1) Hazardous wastes shall be collected, treated, stored and disposed of only in such facilities as may be authorised for this purpose.

(2) Every occupier generating hazardous wastes and having a facility for collection, reception, treatment, transport, storage and disposal of such wastes shall make an application in Form 1 to the State Pollution Control Board for the grant of authorisation for any of the above activities.

Provided that the occupier not having a facility for the collection, reception, treatment, transport, storage and disposal of hazardous wastes shall make an application to the State Pollution Control

Board in Form 1 for the grant of authorisation within a period of six months from the date of commencement of these rules.

(3) Any person who intends to be an operator of a facility for the collection, reception, treatment, transport, storage and disposal of hazardous wastes, shall make an application in Form 1 to the State Pollution Control Board for the grant of authorisation for any of the above activities:

Provided that the operator engaged in the business of collection, reception, treatment, transport, storage and disposal of hazardous wastes shall make an application to the State Pollution Control Board in Form 1 for the grant of authorisation within a period of six months from the date of commencement of these rules.

(4) The State Pollution Control Board shall not issue an authorisation unless it is satisfied that the operator of a facility or an occupier, as the case may be, possesses appropriate facilities, technical capabilities and equipment to handle hazardous wastes safely.

(5) The authorisation to operate a facility shall be issued in Form 2 and shall be subject to conditions laid down therein.

(6) (i) An authorisation granted under this rule shall, unless sooner suspended or cancelled, be in force for a period of two years from the date of issue or from the date of renewal.

(ii) An application for the renewal of an authorisation shall be made in Form 1, before its expiry.

(iii) The authorisation shall continue to be in force until it is renewed or revoked.

(7) The State Pollution Control Board may, after giving reasonable opportunity of being heard to the applicant, refuse to grant any authorisation.

6. Power to Suspend or Cancel An Authorisation

(1) The State Pollution Control Board may cancel an authorisation issued under these rules or suspend if for such period as it thinks fit if, in its opinion, the authorised person has failed to comply with any of the conditions of the authorisation or with any provisions of the Act or these rules, after giving the authorised person an opportunity to show cause and after recording reasons therefor.

(2) Upon suspension or cancellation of the authorisation and during the pendency of an appeal under rule 12, the State Pollution Control Board may give directions to the person whose authorisation has

been suspended or cancelled for the safe storage of the hazardous wastes, and such person shall comply with such directions.

7. Packaging, Labelling and Transport of Hazardous Wastes

(1) Before hazardous waste is delivered at the hazardous wastes site, the occupier or operator of a facility shall ensure that the hazardous waste is packaged in a manner suitable for storage and the labelling and packaging shall be easily visible and be able to withstand physical conditions and climatic factors.

(2) Packaging, labelling and transport of hazardous wastes shall be in accordance with the provisions of the rules issued by the Central Government under the Motor Vehicles Act, 1988, and other guidelines issued from time to time.

8. Inventory of Disposal Sites

(1) The State Government or a person authorised by it shall undertake a continuing programme to identify the sites and compile and publish periodically an inventory of disposal sites within the State for the disposal of hazardous wastes.

(2) The State Government or a person authorised by it shall undertake an environmental impact study before identifying a site as waste disposal site in the State.

(3) The State Government or a person authorised by it shall undertake a continuing programme to compile and publish an inventory of sites within the State at which hazardous wastes have at any time been stored or disposed of and such inventory shall contain, besides the location and description, information relating to the amount nature and toxicity of hazardous wastes at each such site as may be associated with such site.

9. Records and Returns

(1) The occupier generating hazardous waste and operator of a facility for collection, reception, treatment, transport, storage and disposal of hazardous wastes shall maintain records of such operations in Form 3.

(2) The occupier and operator of a facility shall send annual returns to the State Pollution Control Board in Form 4.

10. Accident Reporting and Follow-up

Where an accident occurs at the facility or on a hazardous waste site or during transportation of hazardous wastes, the occupier or operator of a facility shall report immediately to the State Pollution Control Board about the accident in Form 5.

11. Import of Hazardous Wastes

(1) Import of hazardous wastes from any country to India shall be permitted for dumping and disposal of such wastes. However, import of such wastes may be allowed for processing or reuse as raw material, after examining each case in merit by the State Pollution Control Board or by an officer authorised in this behalf.
(2) The exporting country or the exporter, as the case may be, of hazardous waste shall communicate in Form 6 of the Central Government (the Ministry of Environment and Forests) of the proposed transboundary movement of hazardous wastes.
(3) The Central Government shall, after examining the communication received under sub-rule (2) and on being satisfied that the import of such hazardous wastes is to be used for processing or reuse as raw material, grant permission for the import of such wastes subject to such conditions as the Central Government may specify in this behalf and if, however, the Central Government is not satisfied with the communication received under sub-rule (2), it may refuse permission to import such hazardous wastes.
(4) Any importer importing hazardous wastes shall provide necessary information as to the type of hazardous wastes he is to import, in Form 6, to the concerned State Pollution Control Board/ the Central Pollution Control Board in the case of Union Territories.
(5) The State Pollution Control Board shall examine the information received under sub-rule (4) and issue such instructions to the importer as it considers necessary.
(6) The Central Government or the State Pollution Control Board, as the case may be, shall inform the concerned Port Authority to take appropriate steps regarding the safe handling of the hazardous wastes at the time of off-loading the same.
(7) Any person importing hazardous wastes shall maintain the records of the hazardous wastes imported as specified in Form 7 and the records so maintained shall be open for inspection by the State

Pollution Control Board/the Ministry of Environment and Forests/ the Central Pollution Control Boards in the case of Union Territories or an officer appointed by them in this behalf.

12. Appeal

(1) An appeal shall lie, against any order of suspension or cancellation or refusal of an authorisation by the State Pollution Control Board to the State Government and to the Ministry of Environment and Forests in the case of the Central Pollution Control Board.

(2) Every appeal shall be in writing and shall be accompanied by a copy of the order appealed against and shall be presented within thirty days of the order passed.

SCHEDULE

[SEE RULES 3(i), 3(n) AND 4]

CATEGORIES OF HAZARDOUS WASTES

Waste Categories	Types of wastes	Regulatory quantities
1	2	3
Waste Category No. 1	Cyanide wastes.	1 kilogramme per year calculated as cyanide.
Waste Category No. 2	Metal finishing waste.	10 kilogrammes per year the sum of the specified of the substance calculated as pure metal.
Waste Category No. 3	Waste containing water soluble chemical compounds of lead, copper, zinc, chromium, nickel, selenium barium and antimony	10 kilogrammes per year the sum of the specified substance calculated as pure metal.
Waste Category No. 4	Mercury, arsenic thallium & cadmium bearing wastes.	5 kilogrammes per year the sum of the specified substance calculated as pure metal.
Waste Category No. 5	Non-halogenated hydrocarbons including solvents.	200 kilogrammes per year calculated as non-halogenated hydrocarbons.
Waste Category No. 6	Halogenated hydrocarbons including solvents.	50 kilogrammes per year calculated as halogenated hydrocarbons.

Contd . . .

... Contd

Waste Categories	Types of wastes	Regulatory quantities
1	2	3
Waste Category No. 7	Wastes from paints, pigments, glue, varnish & printing ink.	250 kilogrammes per year calculated as oil or oil emulsions.
Waste Category No. 8	Wastes from dyes & dye intermediates containing inorganic chemical compounds.	200 kilogrammes per year calculated as inorganic chemicals.
Waste Category No. 9	Wastes from dyes & dye intermediates containing organic chemical compounds.	50 kilogrammes per year calculated as organic chemicals.
Waste Category No. 10	Waste oil & oil emulsions.	1000 kilogrammes per year calculated as oil and oil emulsions.
Waste Category No. 11	Tarry wastes from refining and tar residues from distillation or pyrolytic treatment.	200 kilogrammes per year calculated as tar.
Waste Category No. 12	Sludges arising from treatment of waste waters containing heavy metals, toxic organics, oils, emulsions and spent chemicals & incineration ash.	Irrespective of any quantity.
Waste Category No. 13	Phenols.	5 kilogrammes per year calculated as phenols.

Contd...

... Contd

Waste Categories	Types of wastes	Regulatory quantities
1	2	3
Waste Category No. 14	Asbestos.	200 kilogrammes per year calculated as asbestos.
Waste Category No. 15	Wastes from manufacturing of pesticides and herbicides and residues from pesticides and herbicides formulation units.	5 kilogrammes per year calculated as pesticides and their immediate products.
Waste Category No. 16	Acid/alkaline/ slurry wastes.	200 kilogrammes per year calculated as acids/alkaline.
Waste Category No. 17	Off-specification and discarded.	Irrespective of any quantity.
Waste Category No. 18	Discarded container & container liners of hazardous & toxic chemicals and wastes.	Irrespective of any quantity.